# INFANT
# MASSAGE

# INFANT MASSAGE
## (Revised)

## A Handbook
## for Loving Parents

### VIMALA SCHNEIDER McCLURE

A
BANTAM
TRADE
PAPERBACK

**BANTAM BOOKS**
NEW YORK · TORONTO · LONDON · SYDNEY · AUCKLAND

INFANT MASSAGE: A HANDBOOK FOR LOVING PARENTS
A Bantam Book / September 1982
Revised Bantam edition / September 1989

PRINTING HISTORY
Originally published by Monterey Laboratories, Inc.
Portions of chapters ten and twelve previously appeared in
Mothering magazine (Summer '86 and Spring '87)

Library of Congress Cataloging-in-Publication Data
McClure, Vimala Schneider, 1952–
Infant massage: a handbook for loving parents/Vimala Schneider
McClure.—Rev. Bantam ed.
p. cm.
Bibliography:p.
ISBN 0-553-34632-6
1. Massage for infants.     I.Title
RJ53M35M33     1989
649'.4—dc20                                88-47844
                                                  CIP

Published simultaneously in the United States and Canada

PRINTED IN THE UNITED STATES OF AMERICA

CW   0 9 8 7 6

# Acknowledgments

Heartfelt thanks to all those who have helped and supported my work over the years. Special thanks to the following people for helping bring this new edition to birth: to Toni Burbank for making it happen; to Jody Wright, Mary Fuhr, Diana Lundgren, and Janet Speirer for help with the chapter on special needs babies; to pediatricians Dr. Jerry Rubin and Dr. Ed Berman for help with the chapters on colicky and premature babies; to all the parents who graciously allowed me to photograph them and their infants; to Peg and John MacMahon, of "Mothering," for providing much inspiration, and to my husband and partner, Michael, whose patience, strength, and assistance brought me through "transition."

I also thank my colleagues and friends in the International Association of Infant Massage Instructors for their hard work, dedication, and service to humanity through this work. It is their realization of its long-range potential which has brought its benefits to so many parents and, I believe, contributed to a significant change in our infant parenting practices.

Frail newborn wings,
Small voice that sings,
New little beating heart,
Dread not thy birth,
Nor fear the earth—
The Infinite thou art.
The sun doth shine
The earth doth spin,
For welcome—enter in
This green and daisied sphere.
Rejoice—and have no fear.
—RICHARD LeGALLIENNE

Dedicated to
P.R. Sarkar

and to my beloved children
Narayana, Sadhana, and Adam

# Contents

Foreword
      by Walt Schafer, Ph.D.                            xiii
Preface
      Stephen Berman, M.D.                              xv
Introduction                                           xvii

WHY MASSAGE YOUR BABY?                                  1
      Benefits of Skin Stimulation                      4
      Stress and Relaxation                             8
      Into Adulthood                                    12

YOUR BABY'S SENSORY WORLD                               15
      Touch and Movement                                15
      Taste and Smell                                   16
      Sight and Hearing                                 16
      The "Infant Stim" Controversy                     19

BONDING AND INFANT MASSAGE                              23
      The Elements of Bonding                           26
      Delayed Bonding                                   29
      Infant Daycare                                    30

ESPECIALLY FOR FATHERS                                  35

HELPING BABY LEARN TO RELAX                             43
      Touch Relaxation Techniques                       45
      How to Use Touch Relaxation                       46
      Are You Relaxed?                                  47

MUSIC AND MASSAGE                                       51

GETTING READY 57
    When and Where? 58
    Warmth 59
    Positioning 60
    What You Need 61
    Which Oils, and Why? 62
    The Massage Technique 64

LET'S BEGIN 67
    Relax and Breathe Fully 68
    Request Permission to Begin 68
    Just the Two of You 70
    The Legs and Feet 71
    The Stomach 80
    The Chest 89
    The Arms 93
    The Face 100
    The Back 105
    Gentle Movements 111
    Review of the Strokes 118
    Abbreviated Massage 121

INFANT COMMUNICATION 123
    Stages of Growth 124
    Fussing 126
    Crying 127
    How to Listen to a Baby 131

ILLNESS AND COLIC 135
    Gas and Colic 136
    A Colic Relief Routine 137

THE PREMATURE BABY                                      141
    Massaging Your Premature Baby in
      the Hospital                                   144
    How to Begin                                     150
    Eye Contact                                      152
    Trouble Spots                                    152
    Massaging Your Baby at Home                      153

MASSAGING THE BABY WITH SPECIAL NEEDS    159
    Developmental Impairments                        161
    Visual Impairments                               168
    Hearing Impairments                              170

THE OLDER CHILD                                        173
    How to Begin                                     175
    Stroke and Movement Modification                 176
    Rhymes and Games for the Older Baby              178
    Helping an Older Child Adjust to a New Baby      185
    Healthy Touching                                 187

References                                             189

# Foreword

Infant Massage is a rare and beautiful gift for young parents, aiding them in their own gift for their young children—caring touch.

Research findings abound showing that the unfolding of human potential depends on a nurturant climate during childhood. Touch, beginning at day one, is a vital component of that climate. And what better method of intimate human contact than daily massage, carefully learned and carefully applied. Vimala Schneider McClure's book, based on years of study, practice, and teaching, aids parents in learning the whys and hows of infant massage.

Research leaves little doubt on another, less pleasant matter. External pressures are sure to mount as we approach the end of this century and prepare for the twenty-first: economic instability, energy shortages, threat of war, pollution, crime, galloping change, and more. Already, experts estimate that stress plays a part in 60 to 90 percent of all illnesses. The threat of ever-mounting stress looms large.

Young adults, then, face twin challenges. First, their own well-being depends upon maintaining a personal buffer against stress. A good buffer includes, for example, regular aerobic exercise, good nutrition, adequate sleep, a social support network, practice of deep relaxation, and clear beliefs and values. Effective stress prevention is identical, then, to effective preventive medicine.

Second, young parents face the growing challenge of preparing their children to flourish in tomorrow's world of pressure and uncertainty. Perhaps a parent's greatest gift is a climate of love, encouragement, and warmth. Such a climate yields fruits of self-esteem and freedom from an unnecessary buildup of body tension. Caring touch through infant massage can prove invaluable, then, not only in healthy personality development, but in early practice of stress control for the child. And mothers and fathers surely will find peace and nurturance for themselves through infant massage.

Vimala Schneider McClure recently came to my hospital-based Stress and Health Center to train ten West Coast instructors in how to teach new mothers techniques of infant massage. I was highly impressed with Vimala's depth of understanding about child development, bonding, human anatomy, stress management, and more. I was even more impressed by the enthusiasm and skill she instilled in her trainees and in mothers who participated with their babies in the weekend. The infants obviously enjoyed the experience.

Fortunately, *Infant Massage* now brings Vimala's teachings to a broader audience. New mothers and fathers will benefit. Their babies will benefit even more, now and in years to come. And since our future rests in their hands, Vimala's book is a gift of love for us all.

Walt Schafer, Ph.D.
Sociology Department Chairman
California State University at Chico
Chico, California

# Preface

During the past two decades physicians have reassessed the importance of maternal-infant bonding in relation to development. Studies conducted at the University of Colorado and elsewhere have demonstrated that infants whose mothers have difficulty in touching, cuddling, or talking to their infants during the first few months of life are more likely to suffer from developmental or growth delay. Scientific advances in the understanding of newborn and infant sensory, motor, and cognitive processes have resulted in new appreciation for many of the cultural parenting practices of the nonindustrialized world. For example, the infant carrier packs such as the Snugli are modeled after practices observed in many parts of Africa and Latin America. These infant carriers promote mutual feelings of comfort and security associated with close body contact and still provide the parent with freedom of movement.

In her book, *Infant Massage: A Handbook for Loving Parents,* Vimala Schneider McClure introduces us to a form of parenting which has been practiced for centuries in India. The value of infant massage as a parenting technique can be appreciated best by recognizing the maternal-infant interaction as displayed in the faces of Vimala and her baby shown in the pictures in this book. Hopefully, parents will accept infant massage into the American way of life in the same way that Lamaze childbirth classes and infant carriers have been accepted. An added plus to infant massage is the opportunity it provides to the father, especially of a breastfed baby, for positive interaction with his child.

As a pediatrician, the best advice I can give you is

to try the techniques described in this book. If the interaction between you and your child is enjoyable and the massage is fun, you will be providing your infant with a pleasurable form of stimulation which may build a strong foundation for your child's development.

Stephen Berman, M.D.
Chief of General Pediatrics
University of Colorado Health Sciences Center

# Introduction

While studying and working in a small orphanage in India in 1973 I made a discovery that was to substantially redirect my life.

I became aware of the importance of the traditional Indian baby massage, both for its soothing effects and for its role in affectionate nonverbal communication. An Indian mother regularly massages everyone in her family and passes these techniques on to her daughters. In the orphanage, the eldest massaged the little ones nearly every day; it was a type of nurturing I hadn't seen in the U.S. I received its benefits when, during my last week in India, I succumbed to malaria. When I was delirious with fever, all the women in the neighborhood came to look after me. They massaged my body as if it were a baby's and sang to me, taking turns until my fever broke. I will never forget the feeling of their hands and hearts touching me.

On my way to the train station after a tearful goodbye at the orphanage, my rickshaw stopped to let a buffalo cart go by. To my right was a shanty—just a few boards and some canvas—where a family lived by the road. A young mother sat in the dirt with her baby across her knees, lovingly massaging him and singing. As I watched her I thought, *There is so much more to life than material wealth.* She had so little, yet she could offer her baby this beautiful gift of love and security, a gift that would help to make him a compassionate human being.

I thought about all the children I had known in India and how loving, warm, and playful they were in spite of their so-called disadvantages. They took care of one another and they accepted responsibility without reservation. Perhaps, I thought, they are able to be so loving, so relaxed and natural because they have been loved like this as infants, and infants have been loved this way in India for thousands of years.

My first child was born in 1976 and I began massaging him every day. Having taught yoga for several years, I found that a number of its massage techniques were easily incorporated into our daily massage routine—a routine based on my own combination of Indian and Swedish methods. This joyful blend provided my son with a wonderful balance of outgoing and incoming energy, of tension release and stimulation. Additionally, it seemed to relieve the painful gas he had been experiencing that first month.

When I massaged my baby, he appeared to relax and was happier for the rest of the day. When I stopped massaging him for two weeks, the change was noticeable. He seemed to carry tension with him and to express more general irritability and fussiness. From that point on I decided that massage would remain a permanent part of our lives—not only as a tool for relaxation, but as a key part of our communication with one another.

When my son was seven months old I decided to develop a curriculum and share my discoveries with other parents. Since then hundreds of parents and infants have participated in my classes and private instruction. Over the years, they have provided me with continuing education and inspiration for which I am most grateful.

In the years since my early classes, interest in infant massage has grown steadily among parents and professionals alike. Our organization, the International Association of Infant Massage Instructors, has trained hundreds of instructors all over the world. Many hospitals now train nursery staff to use massage with premature and sick babies and offer instruction to parents in an effort to promote bonding and ease babies' discomforts. In addition, the benefits of this simple tradition, intuitively developed, are unfolding day by day in scientific research.

My children are grown now, and the impact of our experience with massage during their infancies has not diminished. The daily massages provided a foundation for physical, emotional, and spiritual harmony that we will all carry with us for the rest of our lives.

## ON CHOOSING THE RIGHT WORD

Like many of today's authors I have encountered the male-female pronoun problem. When referring to a baby, do I say "he or she"? Or "he/she"? Or "s/he"? All of these seem clumsy and forced. So, to get my own message across as simply as possible, I have chosen to refer to the baby as "he" some of the time, and "she" some of the time—providing balance for all.

Another problem was in reference to the person massaging the baby. I have used Mother as the primary masseuse in the book both for the sake of convenience, and because, in my experience, she is most often principally involved in this care. However, since it is my sincere hope that fathers may be equally interested and involved, I have included a special section for them. To those fathers who read the book and decide to massage their babies, I would simply ask that, in their minds, they change "Mother" to "Father" at the appropriate places.

Enough said!

Vimala Schneider McClure

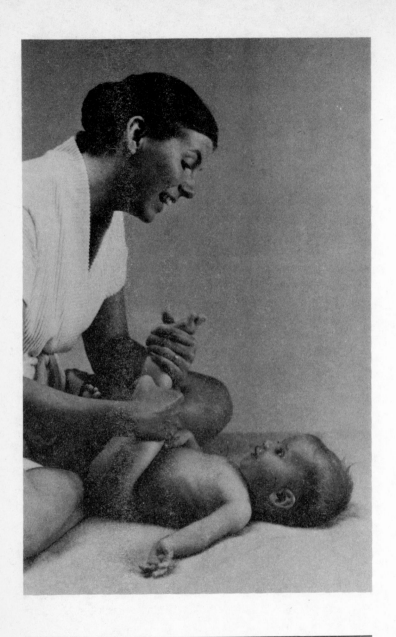

# CHAPTER ONE

# Why Massage Your Baby?

Being touched and caressed,
being massaged, is food for the infant.
Food as necessary as minerals,
vitamins, and proteins.
                              —DR. FREDERICK LEBOYER

A young mother gently cradles her baby in her lap as the afternoon sun breaks through cracks in the wooden door. For the second time that day, she carefully removes the tiny cap and begins to unwrap the swaddling bands of soft white linen and wool.

Free from his snug encasement, the baby kicks and waves his little arms, listening for the now familiar swish-swish of the warm oil in his mother's hands, and the comforting sound of her balmy lullaby. So begins his twice-daily massage.

The scene is in a Jewish *shtetl,* one of the small enclaves in Poland in the early nineteenth century, but we could be anywhere in the world, in any century, for it is a familiar tableau of motherhood in every culture throughout the ages.

From the Eskimos of the Canadian Arctic to the Ganda of East Africa; from South India to Northern Ireland; in Russia and Sweden and South America; in South Sea island huts and modern American homes, babies are lovingly massaged, caressed, and crooned to every day. Mothers all over the world know their babies need to be held, carried, rocked, and fondled. The gentle art of infant massage has been part of baby care-giving traditions passed from parent to child for generations. Asked why, each culture would provide different answers. Most would simply say, "It is our custom."

Many of the family customs of our ancestors, turned aside in the early twentieth century in the interest of "progress," are returning to our lives as modern science rediscovers their importance and their contribution to our infants' well-being and that of whole communities. Cross-cultural studies have demonstrated that in societies where infants are held, massaged, rocked, breastfed, and carried, adults are less aggressive and violent, more cooperative and compassionate. Our great-grandmothers would stand up and utter a great "I told you so!" were they to observe our "new" discoveries in infant care.

Research can help us understand why these traditional practices are so important. Knowing why, we will be less quick to cast adrift customs which can deeply enrich our lives. Nearly every new parent hears the admonition "Don't spoil the baby!" at one time or another in the early months of parenting. Our concern about raising "spoiled" children comes from an earlier time when behaviorists, after discovering behavioral

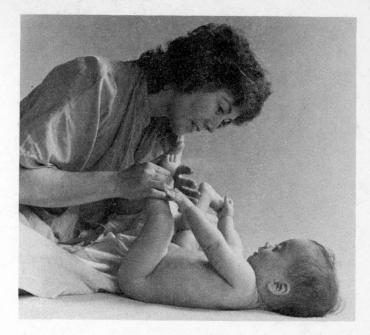

conditioning, thought that we could condition our babies to behave like little adults by ignoring their cries and not offering too much affection. After thirty years of intensive research, it has become obvious that, like fruit, it is neglect rather than attention that spoils a child! "I'd gotten so much pressure about spoiling the baby, even before she was born," says Judith, mother of three-month-old Kelsey. "But I felt differently inside. The information about the benefits of infant massage gave me permission to be the kind of mother I want to be and the research to back me up when I am contradicted." When we know why our caress is so important to our babies, we are more likely to follow our intuition, to relax and give way to our natural inclinations.

Both for babies and parents, the benefits of infant massage are more far-reaching than they may at first seem. For infants, massage is much more than a luxurious, sensual experience or a type of physical therapy. It is a tool for maintaining a child's health and well-being on many levels. It helps parents feel secure in their ability to do something positive for—and get a positive response from—this squealing bit of newborn humanity suddenly and urgently put in their charge.

## THE BENEFITS OF SKIN STIMULATION

Skin sensitivity is one of the earliest developed and most fundamental functions of the body. Stimulation of the skin is, in fact, essential for adequate organic and psychological development, both for animals and human beings. When asked what he thought of infant massage, anthropologist Ashley Montague commented, "People don't realize that communication, for a baby, the first communications it receives and the first language of its development, is through the skin. If only most people had realized this they would have all along given babies the kind of skin stimulation they require."

You may wonder why I started out talking about babies and now quickly switch to animals. It is because scientists have discovered behaviors and responses in animals which often parallel the growth and development of our own young. And these parallels are truly fascinating!

Behaviorally, mammals tend to fall into the "cache" or "carry" type. The caching species leave their young for long periods while the mother gathers food. The infants must remain silent for long periods of time so as not to attract predators, therefore they do not cry. For the same reason they do not urinate unless stimulated by the mother. In addition, the young have internal mechanisms that control their body temperature. The mother's milk is extremely high in protein and fat, and the infants suckle at a very fast rate.

In contrast, the carrying species maintain continuous contact with their infants and feed often. The babies suckle slowly, they urinate often, they cry when distressed or out of contact with the parent, and they need the parent to keep them warm. The mother's milk content is low in protein and fat. Humans are designed like the carrying species; in fact, human milk is identical in protein and fat content to that of the anthropoid apes, a carrying species. Our infants need to be in close physical contact with us as much as possible.

Harry Harlow's famous monkey experiments were the first to show that for infants contact comfort is more important than even food. Infant monkeys given the choice of a wire mother with food or a soft, terrycloth mother without food chose the terrycloth mother figure. Human infants with "failure to thrive" syndrome exhibit the same type of behavior; though given all the food they need, they continue to deteriorate without intervention that involves emotional nurturing, contact comfort, and care.

Physically, massage acts in much the same way in humans as licking does in animals. Animals lick their young and maintain close skin contact. Animals not licked, caressed, and able to cling in infancy grow up scrawny and more vulnerable to stress. They tend to fight with one another and to abuse and neglect their own young. Licking serves to stimulate the physiological systems and to bond the young with the mother. A mother cat spends over fifty percent of her time licking her babies, and you will never see a colicky kitten! In fact, without the kind of stimulation that helps the newborn's gastrointestinal system begin to function properly, kittens die.

In one study, rats with their thyroid and parathyroid (endocrine glands which regulate the immune system) removed responded remarkably to massage. In the experimental group, the rats were gently massaged and spoken to several times a day. They were relaxed and yielding, not easily frightened, and their nervous systems remained stable. The control group rats, which did not receive this type of care, were nervous, fearful, irritable, and enraged; they died within forty-eight hours. Another study with rats showed a higher immunity to disease, faster weight gain, and better neurological development among those gently stroked in infancy.

Moving up the animal scale, dogs, horses, cows, dolphins, and many other animals have also shown remarkable differences when lovingly handled in infancy. Gentle touching and stroking improved the function of virtually all of the sustaining systems (respiratory, circulatory, digestive, eliminative, nervous, and endocrine), and changed behavior patterns drastically, reducing fear and excitement thresholds and increasing gentleness, friendliness, and fearlessness. In his book *Touching,* Dr. Ashley Montague writes, "... the more we learn about the effects of cutaneous [skin] stimulation, the more pervasively significant for healthy development do we find it to be."

In nearly every bird and mammal studied, close physical contact has been found to be essential both to the infant's healthy survival and to the mother's ability to nurture. In the previously mentioned studies with rats, if pregnant females were restrained from licking themselves, their mothering activities were substantially diminished. Additionally, when pregnant female animals were gently stroked every day, their offspring showed higher weight gain and reduced excitability, and the mothers showed greater interest in their offspring, with a more abundant and richer milk supply.

Evidence supports the same conclusions for us humans. Recent studies with premature babies have demonstrated that daily massage is of tremendous benefit. A research project at the University of Miami Medical Center showed remarkable results. Twenty premature babies were massaged three times a day for fifteen minutes each. They averaged 47 percent greater weight gain per day, were more active and alert, and showed more mature neurological development than infants who did not receive massage. In addition, their hospital stay averaged six days less.

Dallas psychologist Ruth Rice conducted a study with premature babies after they had left the hospital. Thirty babies were divided into two groups. The mothers in the control group were instructed in usual newborn care, while the experimental group was taught a daily massage and rocking regime. At four months of age, babies who had been massaged were ahead in both neurological development and weight gain.

The natural sensory stimulation of massage speeds myelination of the brain and nervous system. The myelin sheath is a fatty covering around each nerve, like insulation around an electrical wire. It protects the nervous system and speeds the transmission of impulses from the brain to the rest of the body. The process of coating the nerves is not complete at birth; stimulation speeds this process, thus enhancing rapid neural-cell firing and improving brain-body communication.

In 1978 transcutaneous oxygen monitoring was developed, which enabled physicians to measure oxygen tension in the body through an electrode on the skin. It was discovered that hospitalized infants experience tremendous upheavals in oxygen levels when subjected to stress. Massage has been found to mitigate these fluctuations and is being used in more and more hospitals to help infants maintain a steady state through the stresses of diaper changes, heel-sticks, and other intrusions. New research is demonstrating similar results every day, confirming what age-old tradition has told us: infants need loving touch.

Loving skin contact and massage benefits mothers as well. Mothers who have meaningful skin contact during pregnancy and labor tend to have easier labors and are more responsive to their infants. By regularly massaging your baby (and scheduling yourself for some loving massages during pregnancy), you set up a cycle of healthy responses which improve your mothering skills day by day and enhance your baby's well-being, disposition, and the relationship between the two of you.

## STRESS AND RELAXATION

In our great-grandmother's day, when a baby developed a fever the outcome was uncertain. Each century's children have been plagued with some debilitating disease. Though many contagions have been eliminated through improved environmental conditions and medicine, our century is characterized by a more subtle and insidious malady—stress.

Stress can begin to affect a baby even before he is born. The levels of stress hormones constantly present in a woman's bloodstream directly affect her unborn infant, crossing the placenta to enter his own bloodstream. Studies have shown that prolonged tension and anxiety can hamper a pregnant woman's ability to absorb nourishment. Her baby may be of low birth weight, hyperactive, irritable.

Babies born centuries ago in more primitive cultures had the advantage of extended families, natural environments, and relatively little change. Our children, born into a rapidly advancing technological world, must effectively handle stress if they are to survive and prosper. We certainly cannot eliminate stress, nor would we wish to, for in the proper doses it is an essential component in the growth of intelligence. Let's see how this works.

At times of stress, the pituitary gland produces a hormone, called ACTH (adrenocorticotrophic hormone), which activates the adrenal steroids, organizing the body and brain to deal with an unknown or unpredictable emergency. In experiments on laboratory animals, this hormone has been found to stimulate the production of many new proteins in the liver and brain—proteins which seem to be instrumental in both learning and memory. On being given ACTH, the animals' brains grow millions of new connecting links between the neurons (thinking cells). These links enable the brain to process information.

The stress of meeting unknown situations and converting them into what is known and predictable is essential for our babies' brain development. But stress is only part of the cycle that enhances learning. Without its equally important opposite—relaxation—stress can lead to overstimulation, exhaustion, and shock. When stress piles upon stress without the relief of an equal portion of relaxation, the body begins to shut out all sensory intake and the learning process is completely blocked.

How does this apply to infant massage? First, massage is one way we can provide our children with relaxing experiences. Through the use of conditioned response techniques similar to those developed for childbirth by Lamaze and others, we can teach our babies how to relax their bodies in the face of stress. The ability to relax consciously is a tremendous advantage in coping with the pressures of growing up in modern society. If acquired early in life, the relaxation response can become as much a part of our children's natural systems as the antibodies which protect them from disease.

Stress is a natural part of an infant's life, but often our babies are not able to benefit from it as much as they could. Our fast-paced society overloads babies with input, but it is unacceptable for them to cry to release tension. This double bind leads to many frustrated babies with a lot of pent-up tension and anxiety.

Massage helps babies practice handling input and responding to it with relaxation. Watch an experienced mother massaging her baby. You will see both stress and relaxation in the rhythmic strokes and the baby's reactions. The infant experiences all kinds of new sensations, feelings, odors, sounds, and sights. The rumbles of his tummy, the warm sensation of increased circulation, the movement of air on his bare skin—all are mildly stressful to him. The pleasant tone of his mother's voice, her smile, and her touch are relaxing and relieve the discomfort of encountering these new sensations. She reassures him that the world outside

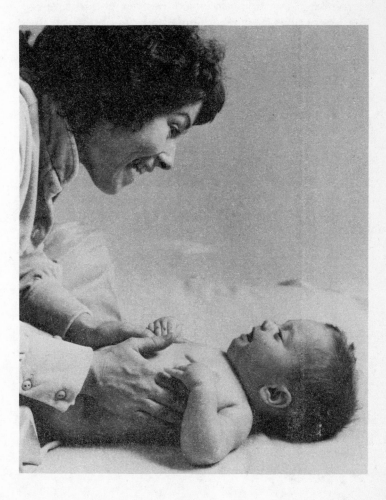

the womb is, as Dr. Frederick Leboyer says, "still alive, and warm, and beating, and friendly."

A daily massage raises an infant's stimulation threshold. Babies who have difficulty handling stimulation gradually build tolerance. High-need babies begin to learn to regulate the manner in which they respond to stressful experiences, which reduces the level of tension they develop throughout the day. Colicky babies are enabled to relax their bodies so that tension doesn't escalate their discomfort. A regular massage provides our babies with an early stress prevention program which will be valuable to them in years to come.

## INTO ADULTHOOD

Recent findings indicate that our adult relationships reflect the type of attachments we formed in our infancy. People whose infancy was secure, who were held and listened to, who had good eye contact with their parents, and who were generally cherished tend to have healthier relationships with others. They believe it's easy to get close to others and have no problem with mutual dependence. They have happy, trusting relationships; their romances last the longest and end in divorce the least often of the groups studied. On the other hand, babies whose attachment bonds are insecure or anxious are later less sympathetic to others and less effective in getting support and help from other people. Their relationships lack trust and intimacy; jealousy, commitment problems, and fears undermine friendships as well as marriages.

The bonds of trust and love, the lessons of compassion, warmth, openness, and respect which are inherent in the massage routine will be carried by your child into adulthood.

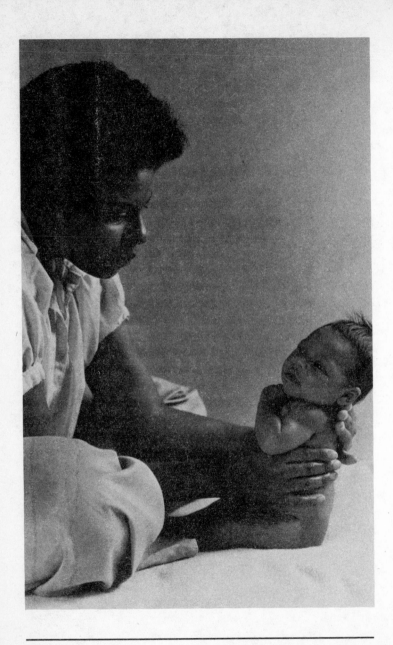

# CHAPTER TWO

# Your Baby's Sensory World

Two little eyes to look around,
Two little ears to hear a sound,
One little nose to smell what's sweet,
One little mouth that likes to eat.
—TRADITIONAL NURSERY RHYME

An infant's senses develop in sequence: first the proximity senses (those which need the nearness of some object to operate effectively), then the distance senses (those which help the baby perceive things which are farther away). Of the proximity senses, the first and most important is touch.

## TOUCH AND MOVEMENT

The sense of touch has been detected in human embryos less than eight weeks old. Though the baby is less than an inch long and has no eyes or ears, her skin sensitivity is already highly developed. Nature begins the baby's massage long before she is born. First the little one rocks and floats, then slowly her world surrounds her ever more closely. The gentle caress of the womb becomes stronger, gradually becoming the contractions which rhythmically squeeze and push, providing massive stimulation to the infant's skin and organ systems.

Infants are accustomed to the tactile stimulation of constant movement and they need the reestablishment of those rhythms after birth. In two recent studies, mothers in one group were asked to carry their infants for extra periods of time each day, in a soft front pack, in addition to carrying during feeding or crying. These infants were compared with infants normally held and carried; at six weeks the infants who received the extra touching and movement cried half as much as the others.

## TASTE AND SMELL

Other proximity senses are taste and smell, both connected with touch and significant to the newborn. A baby only five days old can differentiate her mother's smell and the taste of her milk from that of another mother. Infants, too, have special "chemical signatures" which their mothers are able to detect. Another study showed that mothers could pick out their infants' garments by scent alone after only two hours of exposure to their newborns.

## SIGHT AND HEARING

The distance senses—sight and hearing—can be very important to the baby's emotional attachment to her mother, an attachment which is essential to the development of a healthy parent-baby relationship. However, the blind and/or deaf baby with conscientious

parents will not suffer from lack of this bond; the sense
of touch and its impact upon maternal attachment is
equally powerful. In fact, it may be more dynamic, because it is the most significant and highly developed
sense.

Even before birth, your baby can see. Before you
know you are pregnant, the baby's optic nerve (the
structure which transmits signals from the eye to the
brain) is formed. By six to seven months gestation,
the baby's brain responds to light and she can open
and close her eyes, look up, down, and sideways. Your
newborn is programmed to see you. Her eyes focus
quite clearly at around seven to twelve inches—the dis-

tance at which your arms hold her comfortably. She is especially attracted to the high-contrast, bull's-eye shapes of your eyes and nipples; this attraction enhances bonding through eye and skin contact and thus ensures her survival. In addition, the stimulation of gazing at these objects may enhance nerve myelination and physiological development.

A mother's instinctive use of a high-pitched voice fits in beautifully with her baby's natural attraction to higher frequency speech. The association between auditory and visual centers is fully established as early as two weeks of age. Your baby likes to look at you and hear your voice. In one experiment babies were given four configurations of speech and sight: the mother speaking normally, a stranger speaking normally, a stranger speaking with the mother's voice, and the mother speaking with a stranger's voice. The mother speaking normally was bliss. The babies looked less at a stranger speaking normally. However, the mother-stranger mixes were intolerable and the infants reacted with loud crying whenever they were presented to them. In another experiment newborn infants were fitted with headphones through which they heard a voice telling a story. When they sucked rapidly on a pacifier, they would hear their mothers' voices; otherwise a stranger's voice told the story. The infants learned how to cause their mothers' voices to tell the story, and they preferred their mothers' voices to any other.

The beginnings of language learning can be seen in a baby's movement of her body in rhythm and synchrony with her mother's speech patterns, intonations, and pauses. Computer studies analyzing movies of mothers and babies have revealed that each infant has a unique repertoire of body movements that synchronize with speech—a bodily response to every speech pattern. As the child grows older, these movements become microkinetic—discernible only through sophisticated instrumentation. At first the baby displays constant reflex movements, followed by the development of vocalization, then inflections, emotional content, and babbling. Finally, words come, and ultimately these words have meaning of their own, no longer needing the reflex motor movements. But even a preschool child will move her foot when you ask her to say the word "foot." There is still a trace of the mother's voice, internalized, saying "foot," as the infant body responds. The sounds a mother makes, including "motherese" or baby talk and rhythmic songs and rhymes, appeal directly to the baby's right brain hemisphere, which is more highly developed at this stage. A mother's natural interactions with her baby help her learn in a way that is uniquely suited to her development.

## THE "INFANT STIM" CONTROVERSY

While no one can argue that infants are naturally drawn to the types of stimulation they need for healthy development, there is disagreement about the value of artificially stimulating an infant's senses. Advocates of early stimulation say that looking at stark black and white images (such as mobiles made of black/white bull's-eyes, checkerboards, and stripes), listening to recordings, "white noise" devices (recorded monotonous sounds such as vacuum cleaners and car engines), and other sensory stimuli may speed an infant's development and increase intelligence, help an infant sleep or soothe her colic.

Henry Williams, M.D., consults with parents as chairman of the Anthroposophical Society's Fellowship of Physicians. He proposes that infants have come from a place of soft contours and hazy colors, and that it is reasonable that they be gradually introduced to the hard edges of the world in which they have just arrived. "We want to bring them gently into life on this plane of existence," he says, "to make it a quiet, careful transition with soft music, modified contours, muted colors, slowly introducing them to these edges of things that can be so fascinating because they are new. There is no rush about it."

Our concern about our children competing on intelligence tests can drive us to accept programs that may or may not be valuable and may, in fact, be detrimental to a child's long-range emotional and spiritual development. There is an implication, touted chiefly by makers of products for babies, that our children will not be able to compete for money and status in an increasingly competitive environment unless they are weaned to certain objects and ways of processing information as early as possible. Attaching the infant to material objects as "sensory stimulators" benefits the companies that produce the products and the experts who promote them. On the other hand, parents receive little or no cultural support for their role and are often relieved of stress and guilt by these mechanical interventions. I am concerned about our slowly deteriorating intuitive abilities and confidence in ourselves. We can gradually come to believe that material objects are actually better stimulators, more competent soothers, more efficient brain-developers than we are, and that without these products our babies will be deprived. We spend valuable time that could be spent in emotional nurturing, spiritual teaching, and exploration of the living world working harder and harder to provide the "necessary" objects of stimulation for our infants.

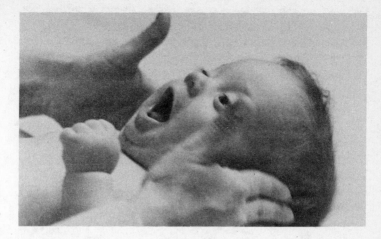

Developmental psychologists today agree that infants are natural learners and will extract from a warm, loving environment whatever information they need. The basic security provided by a strong parent-infant bond enables babies to reach out to their world and to develop to their full capacity physically, mentally, and spiritually. Infant massage provides a wealth of fascinating sensory experiences. Your eyes, your hairline, your smile, your scent, the sound of your voice telling a story or singing a lullaby provide not only the interesting contrast your baby looks for, but also warm, loving feedback. It not only speeds the myelination of her nerves, it lets her know she has come into a living, breathing world. There is no sweeter music than the sound of mother singing; there will never be a toy that can tell a story the way a real, live daddy can. No one has invented a substitute for a parent's loving touch. No vestibular stimulation device can compare with being rocked and carried. And as for white noise, nothing can surpass the sounds of breath and heart in synchrony.

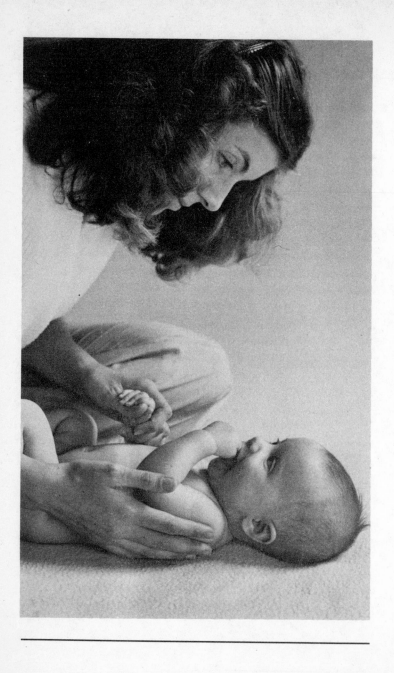

# CHAPTER THREE

# Bonding and Infant Massage

Baby, I lie and gaze on thee
All other things forgot—
In dreams the things of earth pass by,
But awake I heed them not.
I hear thy soft breath come and go,
Thy breath so lately given,
And watch the blue unconscious eyes
Whose light is pure from heaven.

—ANONYMOUS, 1860

Bonding is a basic phenomenon throughout the universe. In terms of physics, it is established within the energy field from which particles arise. Two particles of energy brought into proximity spin and polarize identically, even when separated; two living cells of a human heart brought into proximity begin to beat together. Throughout the animal kingdom and in human life as well, the affectionate and tactile bonds between mother and young ensure healthy interaction and development for time to come. The proximity between parent and infant, via sensory experiences and loving interactions, brings them into an important synchrony with each other.

Animal researchers discovered imprinting long ago. Ethologist Konrad Lorenz showed that ducklings were biologically programmed to follow and bond with the first moving object they saw. Meanwhile, Harry Harlow and his associates studied monkeys and goats and found critical bonding times and elements that were important not only for the infant's physical survival but for what we might call emotional health as well. Monkeys would abuse their infants if their own bonds as infants had been disturbed.

In animals, the crucial period for bonding is usually a matter of minutes or hours after birth. The mother bonds with her infant through licking and touching, a type of massage which, in turn, helps the infant to adjust physically to extrauterine life. If mother and infant are separated during this time and then are subsequently reunited, the mother will often reject or neglect her young. As a result, the newborn may die for lack of the mother's stimulation, even if fed by other means.

In studies paralleling animal research, doctors John Kennell and Marshall Klaus, among others, have revealed that there is also a sensitive period for bonding in humans. However, the critical period seems less rigidly defined and may continue for months, even years, after childbirth. Kennell and Klaus defined bonding as "a unique relationship between two people that is specific and endures through time." They cited cuddling, kissing, and prolonged gazing as indicators of a developing bond. Dramatic evidence in their studies and others correlates the lack of early bonding with later child abuse, neglect, and failure to thrive. Mothers separated from their infants during the newborn period are often more hesitant and clumsy in learning basic mothering tasks. Even very short separations sometimes adversely affect the relationship between mothers and infants.

Experts in many fields are becoming increasingly alarmed at what has been termed "the bonding crisis" in western countries. Dr. Ken Magid, author of *High Risk: Children Without a Conscience,* points to what he calls a "profound demographic revolution" that is changing the course of history. "Working mothers—and the possibility that their children are suffering bonding breaks—are simply not being given enough attention," he says. He cites the stresses of two-income families, an achievement-addicted society, poorly run and understaffed daycare, little or no parental leave in the job market, poorly handled adoptions, and inadequate child custody divorce arrangements as several high risk factors for our newest generations of infants. Unattached and anxiously attached infants grow up to exhibit a range of dysfunctions from difficulty in relationships at one end of the scale all the way to psychopathic criminal behavior at the other.

Unlike the clinging monkey, the human infant has no physical means of initiating contact with his mother and thus getting his needs fulfilled. His life depends upon the strength of his parent's emotional attachment to him. Where there is early and extended mother-baby contact, the studies show impressively positive results. Mothers who bonded with their babies in the first hours and days of life later showed greater closeness to their infants, exhibited much more soothing behavior, maintained more eye contact, and touched their babies more often. Early-contact mothers were more successful in breastfeeding, spent more time looking at their

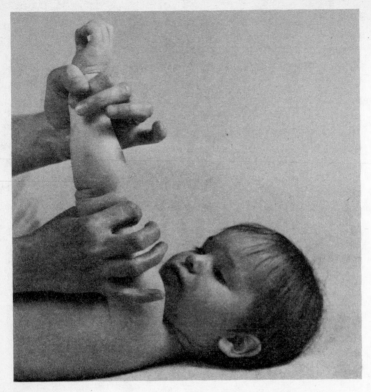

infants during feeding, and their babies' weight gain was greater. These children had significantly higher IQ scores on the Stanford-Binet test at age three than children who had been separated from their mothers.


## THE ELEMENTS OF BONDING


The important elements that help form the bond between parent and infant include eye contact, skin contact, the parent's voice and baby's response to it, odor, rhythms of communication and care-giving, the activation of maternal hormones by contact with the baby, temperature regulation, and the immunizing bacteria and antibodies transferred to the baby by close contact with the mother.

Eye contact is one of the most powerful communication systems we have; between parent and infant, it is a vital connecting link. Parents seem compelled to get into a face-to-face position with their newborns and to gaze into their eyes. New parents croon to their babies, "Come on, now . . . open your eyes. Are you going to look at me?" Delighted exclamations follow when the infant makes eye contact. Mothers report that they first feel really close to their infants when eye contact is made. The baby's visual system is biologically programmed to search out the contrasty bull's-eye shape of the parent's eye and nipple; maternal hormones darken the areola during pregnancy, perhaps to help attract the baby's gaze. Experts speculate that eye contact may be a powerful cue to the infant's physiological system; the message received by the brain allows it to shut down the production of stress hormones initiated during childbirth. During a massage, the infant is positioned face-to-face and the quality of interaction provides a lot of positive feedback, via eye contact, for parent and baby.

Mothers seem to instinctively stroke their babies after birth, bringing myelination to the nerves and awakening the senses. Touch is a very powerful element in human bonding; people in love, children forming friendships, even people who have acquired a new pet will spend extra time in close contact until the bond is secure. Animals raised without touch grow up to be antisocial and aggressive, and they tend to abuse and neglect their young. Neurologist Richard Restak, author of *The Infant Mind,* comments on the importance of touch:

> The infant turns toward the mother. How will she respond? Will she touch him? Will she turn away? How simple the situation, how seemingly devoid of content and importance. But we are deceived by the simplicity of this exchange which takes place within seconds but endures for decades. The mother turns toward her infant and touches him. Neither party speaks. Who could ever have guessed that simply touching another human being could be so important.

A third element in the dance of bonding is vocalization. From the moment he first responded to sound at around seven months gestation, your infant has been listening to your voice. His body moves in rhythm with your speech patterns, and the high-pitched tone you use when talking to him is particularly sweet to his ears. During his daily massage you might sing a song or tell a story. He will come to associate certain sounds with the massage; repeat his name and use the word "relax" to gently teach him how to release tension (we'll cover this more in Chapter Five).

Infant massage helps enhance the bond begun at birth. A baby learns to enjoy the wonderful comfort and security of loving and being loved. He acquires knowledge about his own body as his mother shows him how to relax a tense arm or back, or helps him to release painful gas. Mother looks into his eyes, sings, and talks soothingly as she gently strokes her baby's skin. Thus, each day, the dance of bonding begins all over again. "I feel much closer to my baby and more in tune with her body," says Debbie, mother of three-month-old Kelly. "Knowing that she is growing so fast, it's precious to be able to keep in touch with her little body and experience her growth day by day. I think she feels closer to me also and there is a real trust developing because of our daily massage. I want to treasure her infancy with all its joys and problems; massage is a wonderful way for me to do that. The benefits to my baby—physically and emotionally—are extra gifts."

The daily massage provides a time for a parent to become intimately acquainted with the baby's body language, his rhythms of communication, his thresholds for stimulation, and how his body looks and feels when he is tense or at ease.

Bonding research also points out that parents feel closer to their infants if they can evoke a positive response from a specific series of actions. Massage, which combines intimacy, communication, play, and caregiving, can greatly enhance a parent's feeling of competence. Setting aside a time for touching and caressing, a mother sends her baby a very special message that says, "I love you and want to communicate with you, and you alone." From all my work, I can say that most babies do indeed get the message!

## DELAYED BONDING

Given the appropriate tools and encouragement, a parent and baby can certainly compensate if their bonding has been postponed by separation. If you were not able to establish intimate, affectionate bonds with your baby early on, don't despair. The beauty of the human species is that we have a marvelous ability to overcome setbacks. If you are aware of the importance of these bonds, you can find ways to consciously assist nature. An infant who avoids eye contact, who is stiff and doesn't mold to your body, may need some extra attention and help to begin to trust and form the attachments she needs for healthy development. A daily massage can begin to re-create the elements of bonding that help you get in "sync" with one another. You may find that you must start with very little—perhaps only five minutes—and gradually increase as she begins to accept both your stroking and eye contact. Spending extra time carrying her, sleeping with her, taking baths with her, and playing with her when she is active and alert can help also; whatever activities involve touching, talking, eye contact, and affection are the activities you can focus on.

Some parents find this re-creation difficult because of an overload of stress or depression, which often follow experiences that separate parents and infants. If you feel stressed or depressed, get help now. Counseling can help a great deal; giving voice to your pain is an essential means to healing. A counselor or psychotherapist can also help you to find ways of dealing with stress that you may not have thought about. For your baby's sake, for a long-term healthy relationship between the two of you, outside help can be invaluable.

## INFANT DAYCARE

Experts who have been studying the effects of daycare on babies under a year of age are sounding

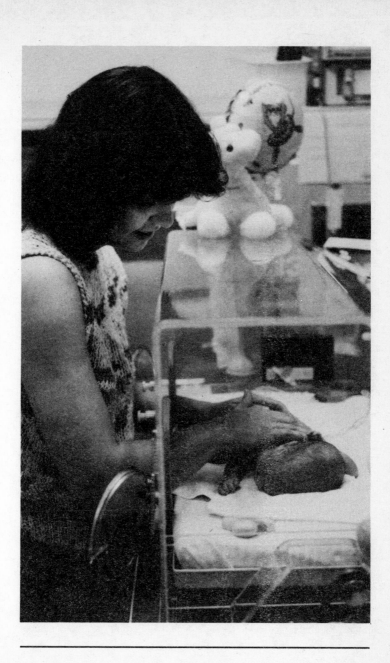

the alarm. Edward F. Zigler of Yale University's Child Development program warned in 1985 that infant daycare is becoming the psychological equivalent to thalidomide*—a powerful statement which, unfortunately, many studies support. Separation from the primary parent too early in life can threaten bonds and wreak havoc on the child's later life and family harmony. Children whose bonding has been anxious or inadequate often grow up with serious psycho-social problems that are difficult to address. Psychologist Ken Magid emphasizes the dangers of too-early daycare in his book *High Risk*. "After reviewing all the literature, it is my opinion that no child should be left for any significant period of time during the first year of life," he says. "Parents of small infants must proceed with extreme caution when they are considering turning care of their baby over to someone else, whether it be a babysitter or relative. These are the most important moments of your baby's life."

Parents who simply cannot take time off from work to care for their newborn infants get little help from our culture in providing substitute care that is of acceptable quality. They must suffer the anguish of separation from their infants, feelings of guilt that result, and worries about the adequacy of the care they have chosen. Often these feelings in themselves serve to distance parents from their infants and further deteriorate the bonds that should be strengthened.

A daily massage can be of tremendous help in maintaining and strengthening affectionate bonds between parents and an infant in daycare. Taking a half hour for reconnecting through massage after work can help a parent focus back on home life and an infant to

---

*A drug given to pregnant women in the late 1950s which caused severe deformities in their developing infants.

feel secure and supported. "Our baby loves his massage and typically smiles and coos throughout," says Barbara, mother of six-month-old John. "Since both my husband and I work, the massage is a way to tune out work and to reconnect with John and each other after a stressful day. We're convinced that our baby is happy and relaxed because of the time we spend massaging him."

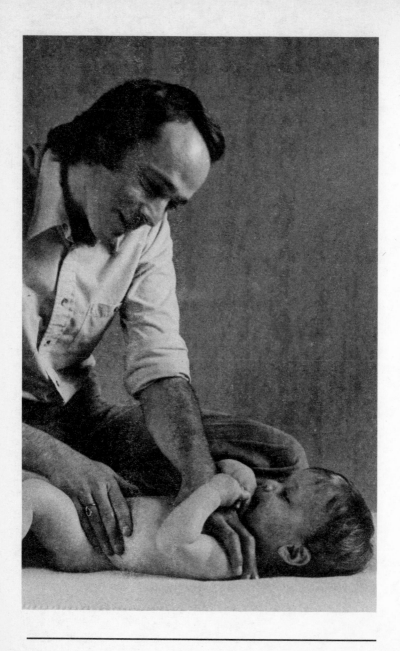

# CHAPTER FOUR

# Especially for Fathers

Our little bud of Paradise
Is wakeful, father. I suppose
His clever brain already knows
That if he bubbles long enough
His head will lean against the rough
Attraction of your overcoat.
—NORMAN GALE

Fathers are taking ever-increasing interest in the active care and nurturing of their infants. The image of the clumsy, frightened father who hands the baby over to his wife until a later, more playful age is fast becoming the exception rather than the rule.

In spite of this eagerness to participate in the baby's care right from the beginning, new fathers may encounter logistical problems. A father's time is usually limited to evenings and weekends. He is often tired after work and now must face the added stress of coping with basic household maintenance and increased financial pressure.

In the first weeks after birth, his wife may be tired at the end of the day and the baby may be fussy. A father is hard-pressed to find time for himself, and may seem withdrawn at times when mother and baby want and need just the opposite response. Of course, his wife is coping with the same problems, compounded by the sometimes overwhelming responsibility of caring for the baby round-the-clock.

This lack of time, along with a lack of learned "maternal" behavior gives fathers two large but hardly insurmountable barriers in learning to nurture their children with soft and gentle care. Because most men have not grown to manhood learning the same behaviors toward babies that most women do, they may need special help and encouragement in the beginning.

Psychologist and infant massage instructor Tom Daly comments, "In the process of giving the massage, fathers get to know their children in an extraordinary way; they connect with a deep part of the child and

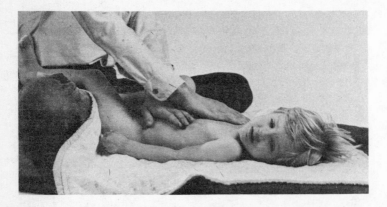

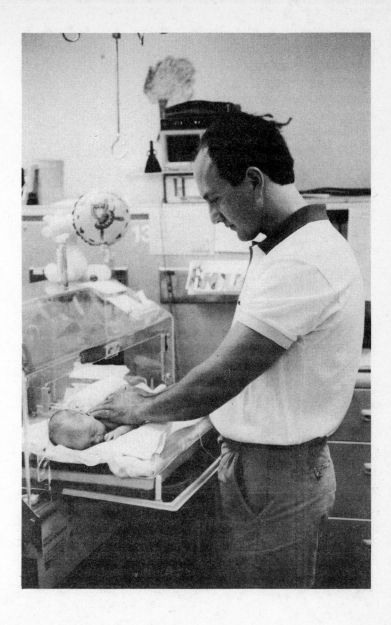

with a deep part of themselves—their nurturing side. Boys, by and large, are conditioned to suppress this part by the age of nine, but working with infants in this way opens up that old place. Dads find they are great nurturers when given a safe situation in which their manhood is not compromised." He notes that children have more self-confidence and exhibit more creativity when their fathers give them extra attention. "Men and manhood are changing," he says. "Let us continue to get fathers more seriously involved in childrearing. Infant massage is a golden opportunity to assist in this transformation. The world is a better place every time an infant is massaged, and men need to be a part of this."

Massage is an excellent tool for the father who wishes to have a whole and healthy bond with his child. Research indicates that infants attach to both parents during the first year of life. A regular massage is an opportunity for a father to have extended contact with his newborn, thus strengthening their attachment to one another.

Children benefit immensely from affectionate interaction with both mother and father. "A warm, affectionate father-son relationship can strengthen a boy's masculine development," says Dr. Michael Lamb, author of *The Role of the Father in Child Development.* "A nurturant father is a more available model than a non-nurturant father. The nurturant father's behavior is more often associated with affection and praise and it acquires more reward value. Thus a boy with a nurturant father has more incentive to imitate his father than a boy with a non-nurturant father." Girls, too, need wholesome bonds with their fathers. The Berkeley Longitudinal Study indicated that the women who were most healthy and well-adjusted as adults grew up in homes

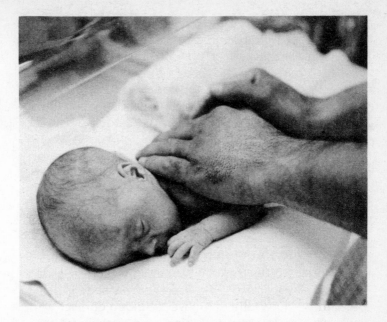

with two loving, involved parents. The most successful women had fathers who valued femininity and encouraged competency, who were warm and affectionate with their daughters and supportive of their efforts toward independence. Massage is a quality experience for both, from which parent and child benefit immensely. The baby learns that Daddy can touch him gently and lovingly; that Daddy, too, is someone he can count on to help meet his physical and emotional needs. A father who realizes these qualities in himself as a result of the massage experience is certain to have his confidence as a parent substantially boosted.

The most important process that evolves from regular massage is the bonding between a father and his newborn. Just as breastfeeding provides consistent reinforcement of the bonding process for mothers, with its cuddling, skin contact, and face-to-face communication, so massaging his baby can be just the thing to keep a father literally in touch with his little one. Fathers who massage their babies regularly throughout infancy recall "massage time" with great fondness. "I'll never forget how my son would wiggle and smile when he heard the oil swishing in my hands," says Ron, father of seven-month-old Jason. "It's going to be fun to tell him about it when he gets older and to remind him of it when he has his own kids. Heck, maybe someday I'll massage his baby, too!"

As a new father, you may have to use some creativity to structure your time to allow for the twenty to thirty minutes you will need to massage your baby. The best time is usually the morning of your day off, when you can relax unhurriedly. After learning the basic techniques from your wife, this book, or a class, you should be alone with your baby for the massage.

In the beginning proceed very gently, massaging only the legs or back. You may have a sense of being too strong, your hands too big or rough, or being too inexpert to massage your baby. Nearly everyone is a little clumsy and nervous in the beginning. Start by gently placing your hands over your baby's back and feeling relaxation and love flow through your hands to your baby. You need not even move your hands in the beginning; just feel the connection between you and your little one, and concentrate on relaxing your body and letting your love go to him. When that feels more comfortable, you can begin a simple stroking, stopping now and then to just hold and relax. Talk or sing softly, make eye contact when baby is ready, and, in general, follow the baby's rhythms of communication. As time goes on and your baby becomes more familiar with your touch, you may want to spend more time and move on to other parts of the body, developing your own special massage techniques. For more ideas and helpful hints, please read on, for this book is meant for you as well.

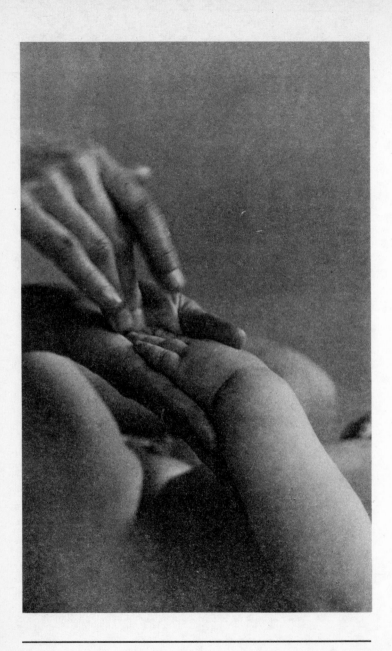

# CHAPTER FIVE

# Helping Baby Learn to Relax

There was a child went forth every day,
And the first object he look'd upon,
    that object he became.

—WALT WHITMAN

Close your eyes for a moment and picture your baby. What do you see? Is she awake or sleeping? Crying? Active or placid? Is she tense or relaxed? Chubby or thin? How does your mental image of your baby compare with the way she really is right now?

Often we unconsciously form images of ourselves and others, including our children, which are based upon limited experience. For instance, my second baby was ill and hospitalized for a little while just after she was born. She came home with a clean bill of health, but for a long time I subconsciously pictured her fragile and weak. Even when I realized that I still carried my early fears and projected them to her, it was difficult to change that image. It had become a habit. These habits of thinking can directly affect those we think about, especially our children, who depend upon us for a clear reflection of themselves.

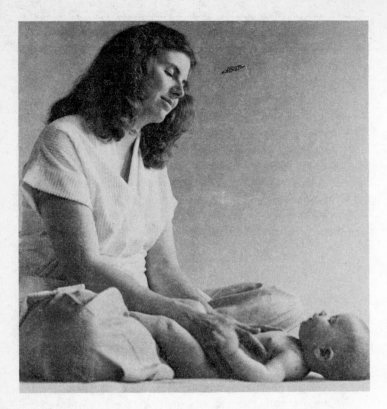

As our thinking is translated into words and actions, the baby adopts these as her own. Positive visualizations and affirmations can help free us from limiting concepts and give our infants the feedback they need to develop to their full potential. The daily massage is a perfect opportunity to practice positive imagery and verbal feedback. As you massage your baby, picture her relaxing, opening, letting go of tension. Visualize her happy and healthy. Try to picture her internal organs as you massage; see her heart beating, her lungs healthy, her intestinal system functioning, gas bubbles moving down and out. Imagine the blood as it moves through her veins and arteries. See your massage facilitating the blood flow to the extremities. Praise her relaxation, her beautiful smile, the softness of her skin. Here are a few examples of statements that help babies adopt positive attitudes about themselves:

"How nice and soft your tummy is!"

"I can feel the gas bubbles moving. Can you help push them out?"

"You are learning how to relax your legs. That's wonderful!"

"Ah, so relaxed, so loose. You feel so happy now."

"Sarah helps Mommy massage. Such a big girl!"

## TOUCH RELAXATION TECHNIQUES

One of the best things a parent can do for her child is to teach her to help herself. The ability to relax completely is a skill we all could use, and the earlier your child learns it, the more naturally it will come when she needs it. One of the benefits of daily massage I have seen in my children is the relaxed way they carry themselves. They were ideal "demonstration models" in my classes because they knew how to relax, even as active preschoolers. Children who have been taught Touch Relaxation techniques in infancy continue to respond as they get older.

My eight-year-old daughter was having several teeth pulled in preparation for orthodontia. It was a frightening and painful experience; I could hear her cries from the dentist's waiting room. I went to her and insisted that the dentist allow me to stay with her during the procedure. He was skeptical, but because she was so upset he was willing to give it a try. I sat down beside her and began massaging her hands and using the gentle bouncing, patting, shaking techniques I had developed for infants. I spoke to her in the high-pitched "Mommy" voice I had used in her infancy and had her take a few deep breaths, close her eyes, and imagine she was floating on a cloud with the warm sun shining on her. She instantaneously relaxed her entire body and the dentist was able to proceed without any further difficulties. I told her that her kitten, Blackie, would come and rub up against her each time she needed to relax more deeply. When I sensed her getting tense again, I would quietly say, "Here comes Blackie," and massage her hand, and her body would go limp again. The techniques of Touch Relaxation have been extremely useful for all of my children's growing-up years. Physical stresses such as illness or injury, emotional stresses such as the first day of school or the loss of a pet, environmental tension such as the transition to a new home—all have been situations in which relaxation techniques were invaluable.

## HOW TO USE TOUCH RELAXATION

The techniques which I call Touch Relaxation are simple and easy to do. They fit in beautifully with the massage routine, but can also be done at other times. If you attended childbirth preparation classes you may remember how you consciously rehearsed relaxing each part of your body. You'll be using a similar principle with your baby, calling her attention to an area, showing her how to relax it, then giving her positive feedback as she learns.

For example, let's say you are beginning to massage the baby's leg and it appears stiff and tense. Take the leg gently in your hands, encompassing and molding your hand to your baby's leg. Feel a heavy relaxation in your hand as it conforms to your baby's skin. Now, gently bounce the leg, repeating in a soft voice, "Relax." Use the same tone each time you say this. As soon as you feel any relaxation in the muscles, give the baby some feedback, saying, "Wonderful! You relaxed your leg." Then offer a smile and a kiss. The same thing can be done with other parts of the body. Use very gentle shaking, patting, encompassing, rolling motions to loosen up the tense area, giving positive feedback when you get a favorable response. Not only will this help baby focus her attention on her own body so that later she knows how to relax herself, it will also help her to associate your touch with the positive benefits of relaxation. In a later chapter, we'll discuss how to use these benefits throughout your baby's childhood years.

## ARE YOU RELAXED?

The first few months of your baby's life are happy and exciting, but they can also be stressful. Right now, take an inventory of your body. Which areas are tense? Are you breathing deeply and fully? Perhaps you are holding your baby, nursing, or walking about as you read. Is your baby fussy? When she cries, what happens to your body? Do you tense up, hold your breath? If your baby is sleeping, are you anxious or restive, partially alert for her cries?

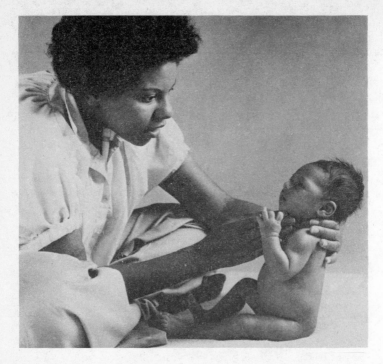

The miraculous changes you have undergone during pregnancy and delivery, the demands of caring for a new baby, the lack of sleep and quiet time, all add up to tension and anxiety which can become habitual in the early weeks and months of parenthood. Your baby's daily massage offers a time to relax and unwind. In fact, a relaxed state of mind is essential.

At one time or another, every mother has felt tense and nervous, and in spite of her best efforts baby begins to fuss and cry. Babies are wonderfully sensitive little beings who pick up every nuance of your communication. If you say "relax" with a furrowed brow, baby will get both messages, but the furrowed brow is much more meaningful to her than your words.

Perhaps your baby has a fussy period during the day or evening. Massage her an hour or so before it usually begins in order to provide her with an outlet for built-up tensions. You will find a simple fifteen-minute massage a welcome respite and transition for the fussy baby/tense mother cycle.

In my son's early infancy, I discovered that massaging him, followed by our taking a warm bath together, helped both of us avoid late afternoon irritability. In the summertime, a massage in the warm morning sun and a splash in the wading pool gave me time for quiet meditation and afforded my baby a wonderful sensory experience.

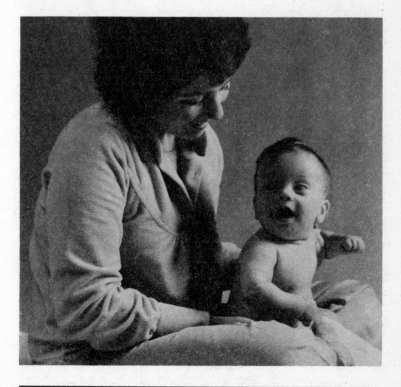

# CHAPTER SIX

# Music and Massage

Upon what Instrument are we two spanned?
And what player has us in his hand?
O sweet song.

—RAINER MARIA RILKE

Your voice can be an important part of your baby's massage. By talking softly, humming, or singing, you create an atmosphere of calm; this verbal communication will also help you keep your mind in the present and your attention on the baby.

Singing is a wonderful way to relax. Sing to your baby any time—changing diapers, feeding, rocking, or walking. You will discover there are some songs your baby loves to hear again and again. His sense of musical discrimination will astound you!

Familiar lullabies from your own childhood would fit in beautifully here. Think of your grandmother's music box that played Brahms's "Lullaby," or the wonderful, lilting "Alouette" you learned in elementary school.

Recall how your own mother sang "Go to Sleep My Baby" to your younger brothers or sisters, and do likewise with your infant.

Here are some folk lullabies from around the world. Undoubtedly you have some family favorites to add to this collection.

Hushabye

American

Hush - a - bye don't you cry, Go to sleep-y lit - tle ba - by. When you wake you shall take all the pret - ty lit - tle po - nies. Blacks and bays, dapples and grays, all the pret - ty lit - tle po - nies.

The following is a Bengali chant from India which means, "I love you, my dear baby." Its wonderfully soothing effect on babies has made it a favorite in our infant massage classes. The words are pronounced: Ah-mee toe-mah-kay, bah-lo bah-shee baby.

A - mi to - ma - ke ba - lo ba - shi ba - by. (repeat)

A - mi to - ma - ke ba - lo ba - shi ba - by. (repeat)

## Schlaf, Kindlein, Schlaf
German

Schlaf kind - lein --- schlaf, Der Va - ter, hüt --- die ---
Sleep ba - by --- sleep. Your fa-ther tends his ---

schaf. Die Mut - ter schuttelts Bau - me - lein, da
sheep. Your mother shakes the dream-land tree, down

fallt her ab ein trau - me - lein. Schlaf kind - lein schlaf.
falls a lit - tle dream for thee. Sleep, ba - by sleep.

## Bayushka Bayu
Russian

1. Go to sleep my dar-ling ba - by, ba - yush - ka ba - yu.
2. I will tell you man - y stor-ies, if you close your eyes.

See the moon is shining on you, ba - yushka ba - yu.
Go to sleep my darling ba - by, ba - yushka ba - yu.

53

## Lullaby

*Japanese*

Shi ba no    o - ri-do - no    shizu - ga - ya    ni
In a hum - ble    lit-tle cot-tage    with a brush wood gate

O-ki - na to    O---u---na ga    su - mai ke --- ri
An old man and    his good wife lived    in a simple    state.

2. Okina wa yama ni      On the mountain every morning
   Shibakari ni              He went gathering wood
   Ouna wa kawa ni        While his old wife washed kimonos
   Kinu susugi.               In the river's flood.

## Arrullo Mi Niño

*Spanish*

Ar - ru - lo mi    ni - ño,    ar - ru --- lo mi    sol.
Lullaby my    ba - by,    lullaby    my    sun.

Ar - ru - lo pe - da - zo    de mi cor - a - zón.
Lullaby lit - tle piece    of your moth - er's heart.

2. Este niño lindo       This pretty little child
   no quiere dormir,     just won't go to sleep,
   el pícaro sueño      that old rascal sleep
   no quiere a venir     just won't come along.

## Dors, Mon Petit Enfant

*French*

Dors    mon pe ---- tit en ---- fant,    dors
Sleep,    lit - tle ba - by    mine,    sleep

dans ton  lit  tout  blanc, som - meil  bien - tot  va
in   your  cra - dle  fine,   slum - ber  soon  will

re ------- ve - nir,  l'en - fant  ché - ri------ va
come      a - gain, dear   ba - by   close  your

s'en---- dor - mir.  Do ---  do  pe - ti --------- te,
eye - lids  then.   Hush,   hush my  lit - tle  one,

do - do  bien  vi - te.  Do-do.
hush, hush  the  day is done.  hush, hush.

If you are not comfortable singing, simply tell a little story, or talk about the massage as you go. It is the tone of your voice that is most important, not the quality of the words and music you project!

Fathers often find the massage time a pleasant opportunity to play tapes or records or fine radio music for background music. Guitar music, pleasant rhythmic tunes which inspire smooth movements, seem to work best.

Perhaps you have some music in your household that would offer an accompaniment to your baby's massage. A soft symphony, the cosmic sound of Paul Horn's flute, a slow raga of Indian sitar, or the sound of ocean waves would all provide a beautiful background for your loving touch.

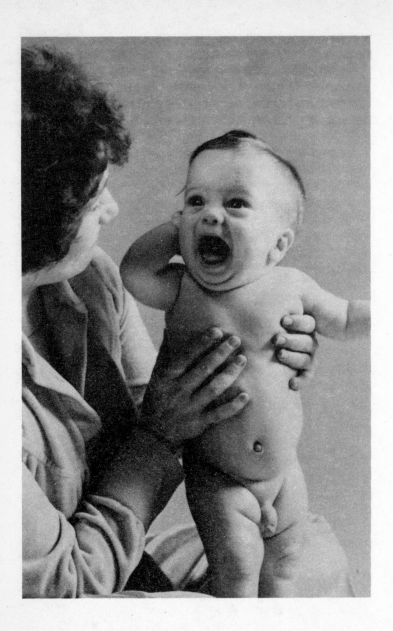

# CHAPTER SEVEN

# Getting Ready

O young thing, your mother's lovely armful!
How sweet the fragrance of your body!
—EURIPIDES

E ven without conscious awareness, a mother will usually begin massaging her baby, ever so gently, from the moment of birth. It is part of the bonding process—a biological urge to know her baby through all of her senses.

The massage in this book can be started as soon as parents desire. The baby will benefit most by a daily massage for the first six or seven months. As the child becomes more active through crawling or walking, this may be reduced to once or twice a week, as desired. A toddler may enjoy a rubdown before bedtime every night, or after bath time. In this case, it should certainly be continued.

# WHEN AND WHERE?

You will want to experiment to find out the time and place that are best for you and your baby. Generally, the morning is a good time to begin, when both of you have been fed and are ready for the day. However, there are also advantages to afternoon and evening massages. For some babies, a massage before a nap is good for releasing that last bit of energy so they can sleep more soundly. For some, however, there is a point of no return—when any stimulation is too much and all the child needs is rest. In this case, give the massage right after the nap. The evening is also a good time for some; if baby is tired but not too cranky, it might also help him to sleep. Your schedule must also be considered. You may work outside the home or have other small children to care for. The evening may be the best time for you, when the day's work is done and your husband can watch the other children for a few minutes. A massage will give you and your new baby the time together that you both deserve.

In the early months, a delightful routine is to massage the baby, then fill a warm bath, and take him in with you. The bath then becomes a wonderfully relaxing experience, and baby may even fall asleep in your arms. To the infant, the experience is rather like a "womb with a view" in that he floats in the womblike warm water, yet, at the same time, sees you as you support him with comfort and security. Baby may cry when you take him out of the tub, but usually some cuddling and/or nursing will quiet him. You may even wish to combine the massage and the bath, massaging him in the tub, using a mild soap instead of oil.

You're probably wondering how both of you get out

of the tub safely and without becoming chilled. My method is to keep an infant seat covered with towels next to the tub, and, when you are ready to get out, put the baby in the seat, wrapping him with the towels. Then you can both crawl into bed for a nap or get going with your day.

From six months of age onward, when bath time becomes more of a playtime for baby, the massage works better after the bath, when he is a little more tired and almost ready for a nap. The massage can help him release that last bit of tension so he can sleep deeply.

Always massage in a warm, quiet place. In the summer, try experiencing the warm morning sun, the sounds of birds, and the smell and feel of the summer air. Take the baby to the beach and massage him with the sound of the water nearby. But take your time . . . your baby is only a baby once.

# WARMTH

Peter Wolff, a well-known pediatrician and researcher who completed many studies of newborns and their behavior, observed that temperature has an important effect on the amount of time babies sleep, on their activity and crying. He found that babies kept at warmer temperatures cried less and slept more than those subjected to cooler environments.

Rudolf Steiner, philosopher, scientist, educator, and propounder of Waldorf Education, also stressed the importance of keeping babies warm. He asserted that the formative forces, both physical and spiritual, which

work to help the babies' bodies and souls grow properly, need this warmth to be effective.

I have observed that babies in our infant massage
classes, especially those under three months of age,
are much more comfortable, startle less and relax more
easily if they are kept quite warm. If your room is cool,
you may want to place a small portable heater nearby.
Or you can wrap a baby-size warm water bottle in a
towel and tuck it under the blanket near the baby's feet
for the massage. The room should be warm enough
so that you can wear light clothing and still feel warm.
Remember, your baby has much less bulk to warm
him, and without clothing he could be chilled easily.


## POSITIONING


Find a comfortable sitting position for massaging
your baby. Your back should be relatively straight, with
most of your movement coming from your lower back
as a "center." You can sit on the floor or a bed with
baby in front of you on a padded pillow or blanket. If
this is uncomfortable, you can stand before a table
or sit propped by pillows or furniture. The cross-legged
position is ideal, for it allows movement, rhythm, and
the proper distance between you and baby.

During the newborn period, the position I call the
"cradle pose" is best. Here's how: Sit on the floor with
legs stretched out, back supported against furniture. Now
bend your knees slightly outward, touching the soles
of your feet together. Pad this area with thick blankets,
making an indentation in the middle for your baby.
Place baby in the "cradle" of your legs, facing you. This

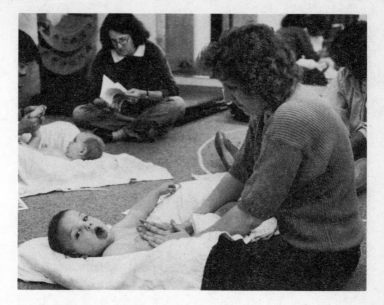

position helps the baby feel more securely positioned and helps conserve warmth. Because babies have the tonic neck reflex for the first four to six months, it is natural, when lying flat, for them to look off to the side. The angle of your legs helps tip baby up slightly toward you; the baby's head can be placed at the arches of your feet, which will help keep his head aligned for eye contact.

## WHAT YOU NEED

Assemble massage oil (which we'll talk about next), towels, a few extra diapers, and a change of clothes for baby. Remember to warm the area, wash your hands, and relax your body before beginning.

# WHICH OILS, AND WHY?

As your hands glide over baby's delicate skin, the last thing you want to do is to create any sort of friction.

Most of the time, you will need a light natural oil to work with. The only exception to this might be where baby's skin is very dry, and an oil-based lotion which absorbs into the skin may help soften more easily. But for regular massages, oil is better than lotion because lotions tend to soak into the skin quite rapidly, which means you would constantly have to stop the massage in order to reapply it.

The primary benefit of oil is that it makes the movement smoother on baby's skin. As you are working, you apply the oil generously to your hands. What kind of oil will do the most good for baby, and enhance the stimulating, yet relaxing effects of the massage itself?

For a number of reasons, I prefer cold-pressed fruit and/or vegetable oils, and stay completely away from the mass-produced heavily advertised "baby oils."

From my research in this area, I have developed the belief that a significant amount of what we put on our skin may actually be absorbed deep within the body. If such is the case, then we quite naturally want to try to nourish our little ones topically, and not use a product that may actually rob them of vital nutrients.

Mass-produced "baby oils" have a nonorganic, nonfood petroleum base. Their primary ingredient is mineral oil. To get mineral oil, gasoline and kerosene are removed from the crude petroleum by heating, in a method called functional distillation. By using sulfuric acid, applying absorbents, and washing with solvents and alkalis, hydrocarbons and other chemicals are then removed.

Not only is there no food value in this type of oil, but it is my personal belief that such a product may actually deplete the system of a number of vitamins, including A, D, E, and K. Some authorities believe that mineral oil, when ingested, produces deficiencies of these vitamins and specifically recommend against its use as a baby oil. Certainly, when you're in the middle of the massage and the baby puts his hand in or near his mouth, you don't want to worry that such a nonfood substance is passing into his delicate digestive system. Infants are particularly vulnerable to substances absorbed by the skin, at a time when their brains and nervous systems are not fully developed. Commercially produced mineral-type baby oils also dry the skin and clog its pores; most modern pediatricians discourage its use for this reason alone.

In India, I saw mothers varying the oils they used to massage their children by the season. In winter, they used hardy mustard oil to conserve warmth. During the summer, they switched to coconut oil for cooling. Apricot kernel and almond oils are two of my personal favorites because of their light, smooth feel and the fact that they absorb readily. Not only do such oils keep their vitamins and minerals intact, but also the fatty acids which contribute to healthier skin. Since these oils are nondrying, they nurture and moisturize the skin rather than deplete it.

Such oils are best when used as close to their natural state as possible. For this reason, you might look for the words "cold pressed" on the label. This means that the oil has been extracted only through the use of pressure, without using heat or solvents, which drastically change and remove the natural nutrients of the oil.

If the oil you select is enhanced with vitamin E, so

much the better, since this vitamin has been shown to be especially good for the skin. It is also a natural antioxidant, which means that it inhibits the product from rancidity. Cold-pressed oils keep the vitamin E intact; refining through heating or other procedures tends to destroy it.

Odor is an often overlooked part of the bonding process. An infant's olfactory system is ready to function as early as seventeen weeks gestation, so it must be an important function for the newborn. A highly refined sense of smell immediately following birth helps a baby discriminate his mother's chemical "signature." Unfortunately, we often assault our infant's senses with noxious smells and thus inhibit this means of bonding. For this reason, I recommend that you use an unscented oil for your baby's massage.

Watch your baby's skin for any reaction to the oil. Some babies exhibit a slight allergy to nut oils, in which case you'd want to switch to safflower or avocado oil. Regular bathing keeps baby's pores from clogging and rashes from developing.

## THE MASSAGE TECHNIQUE

The massage given here is not manipulative in the way an adult massage by a professional masseur may be; no vigorous kneading here. This massage is a gentle, warm communication. A baby's muscles, comprising only a quarter of his total weight (as compared to almost half in adulthood), aren't developed enough to have knots of tension. His body is so tiny that a short, gentle effleurage is enough to stimulate circulation and tone the internal functions.

In the beginning, while you are learning and your baby is tiny, be very soft and gentle. As baby grows stronger, so should your touch. Do not be afraid to touch your baby firmly; you will find she enjoys being handled and massaged in a manner that communicates your strength, love, and confidence. All of your strokes should be long, slow, and rhythmic, with just enough pressure to be comfortable but stimulating.

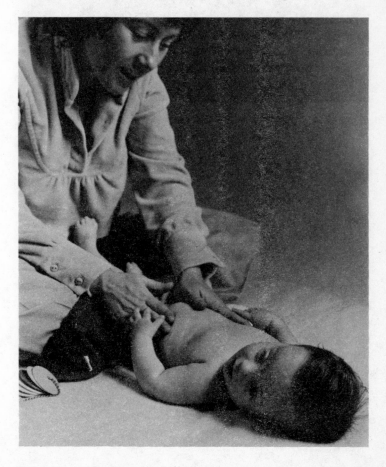

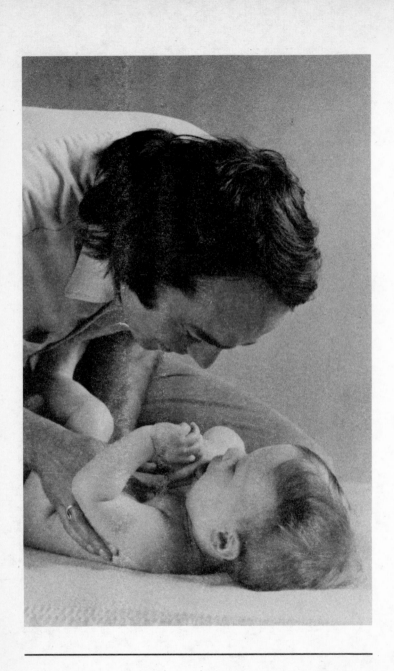

# CHAPTER EIGHT

# Let's Begin

When from the wearying war of life
I seek release,
I look into my baby's face
And there find peace.

—MARTHA F. CROW

When you have assembled your tools, find a comfortable spot for the two of you. Then take a few minutes to sit quietly, with your eyes closed or looking at your baby. Starting at the top of your head, relax every muscle in your body as much as possible. Feel the wave of relaxation wash over you, from your head to the tips of your toes.

Now gently let your head fall forward so that your chin touches your chest. Slowly rotate your head, first clockwise, then counterclockwise, stretching your neck so that your head sweeps in complete, wide slow circles. Feel all the muscles in your neck and shoulders stretch and relax.

# RELAX AND BREATHE FULLY

A harmonious mind parallels slow, deep, and regular breathing. As you massage your baby, breathe deeply and slowly so that your lungs fill with air and exhalation is complete. Once in a while, take an audible sigh, breathing in through your nose and exhaling through your mouth, at the same time you consciously relax your body. Your baby will feel this and eventually begin to imitate your relaxing sighs.

Before you begin, take three deep breaths. With the first breath, affirm, "I now let go of tension. My body is relaxed." Feel all traces of tension or anxiety leave your body. You are confident and centered.

With the next breath, affirm, "I release all other thoughts and focus on my baby." Let all worries and plans leave your mind, like birds flying through a clear blue sky. You are here, now—just you and your baby. You deserve this time together.

Breathe deeply again, and affirm, "I am the gentle power of love, flowing through my hands to my baby." Visualize all the love you feel for your baby as a brilliant sun in the center of your heart. With each heartbeat, its warm radiance courses through your arms, into your hands, and over your baby as you begin the massage.


# REQUEST PERMISSION TO BEGIN

When you are relaxed, focused, and ready to begin, remove your baby's clothing. As you do, tell him that it is massage time and give him a special "cue" that

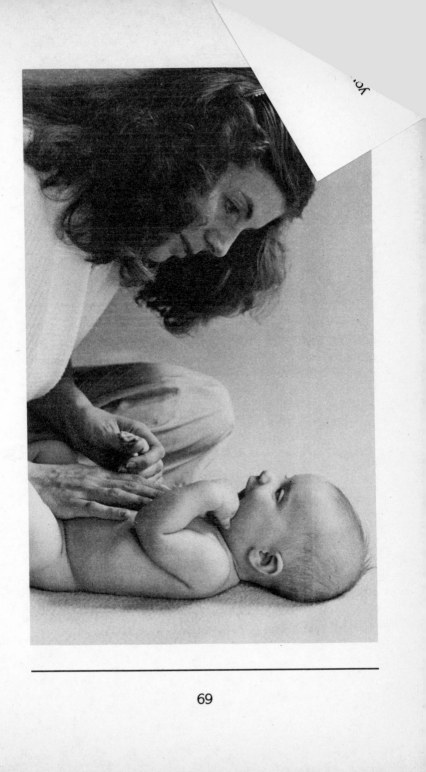

are about to start. Here's how: Pour a small amount of massage oil into your palm. Now rub your palms together to warm them, saying, "It's time for a massage." Your baby will hear the oil swishing between your hands and alert to the sound. Show your palms to baby, saying, "May I massage you now?" The first time, of course, baby doesn't know what is about to happen. However, this routine will, in subsequent sessions, become a cue to which he will respond.

This preparatory routine serves several important purposes. It lets the baby know that a new experience is about to begin and helps him to get ready for it. It also communicates—through your voice and your body language—respect for him. It says, "You are worthy of respect. You are in charge of your body and people should ask your permission to interact with you in this way." Later, in Chapter Thirteen, we will discuss how these early experiences can help your child know the difference between healthy and unhealthy touching as she grows older. Using these cues before beginning a massage now will help build the trust, respect, and values that will ensure a healthy life.

## JUST THE TWO OF YOU

As you massage your baby, every movement of your body will be an expression of your love. Your strong, gentle touch, the rhythm you create, the way you move back and forth with each stroke, your eyes, your smile, your voice, are all as much a part of the experience as the massage itself. Gaze into your baby's eyes and open yourself to the love you share.

# The Legs and Feet

We begin with the legs and feet for several reasons. Babies reach out to the world with their legs and
feet. Observe your baby closely when interacting with
new people. Most infants will wiggle their feet and legs
before making eye contact. Indeed, you may detect a
kind of sign language your baby uses with her feet to
make contact with other people and establish trust.

The feet and legs are the least vulnerable parts of

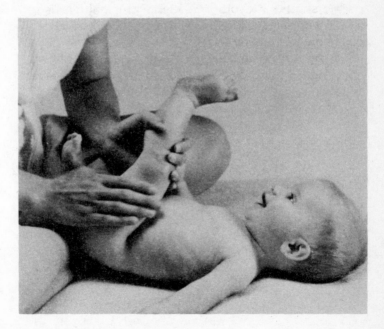

your baby's body. She may become tense or anxious if, right at first, you begin massaging her upper body. She will instinctively "close" her arms and legs to protect her vital organs. Beginning with the legs and feet gives her a chance to establish trust and accept the massage gradually.

For many babies, the legs and feet are the most pleasurable part of the massage. Thus, beginning with the legs helps baby to relax all over.

If your baby has been hospitalized for any reason, she probably received several heel-sticks when hospital personnel drew blood for testing. Sensitivity in this area can remain long after bruises have disappeared. If your baby seems to react with fear or displeasure when you begin to massage her foot, stop using the strokes and simply hold her foot gently in your palms. Use Touch Relaxation for a few days to help her accept touch, then try stroking again.

The "Milking" strokes aid circulation to the feet and back toward the heart. The "Squeeze and Twist" and "Rolling" strokes help tone and relax the legs.

Massage one leg completely, then the other.

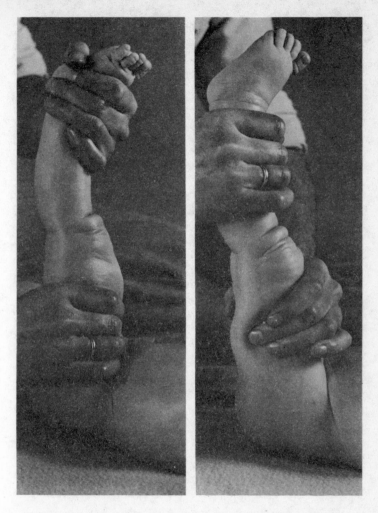

1. *"INDIAN MILKING."* Milk the leg with the inside edge of each hand, one following the other. The opposite hand gently holds the foot at the ankle. The outside hand should move over the buttock; the inside hand moves inside the thigh and up the leg to the foot.

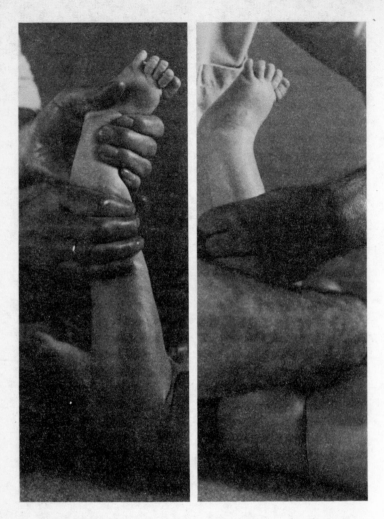

2. *"SQUEEZE AND TWIST."* Hold the leg as if you were holding a baseball bat. Then move hands up the leg together, turning in opposite directions, and squeezing slightly.

3. Push the bottom of the foot from heel to toe with your thumbs, one after another.

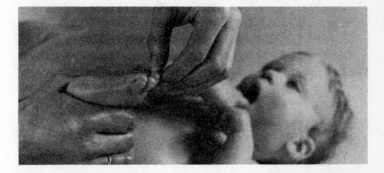

4. Squeeze each toe.

There are seventy-two thousand nerve endings in each foot. The many theories on how foot massage works all agree that points on the feet connect with other body areas. Environmental stresses can cause imbalances in our systems which we experience as colds, flu, ear infections, and so forth. Reflexologists (those who study and work these points on the feet) say that by-products of these imbalances, uric acid and excess calcium, crystallize around nerve endings in the feet, blocking the flow of energy through the body. Foot massage, they say, crushes these crystals so that the excess calcium and uric acid are absorbed by the blood and lymph and eventually excreted out of the body.

5. Pull back gently on the balls of the foot.

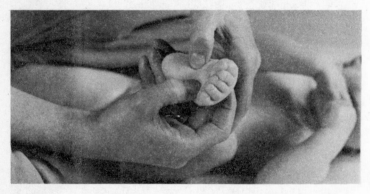

6. Press in with your thumbs all over the bottom of the foot.

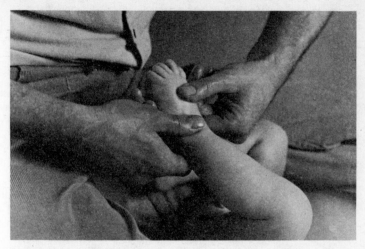

7. Using your thumbs, push the top of the foot toward the ankle.

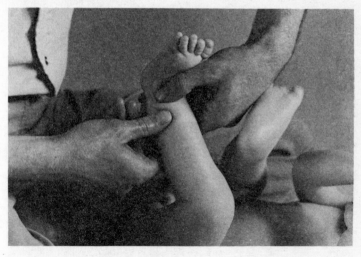

8. Make small circles all around the ankle with your thumbs.

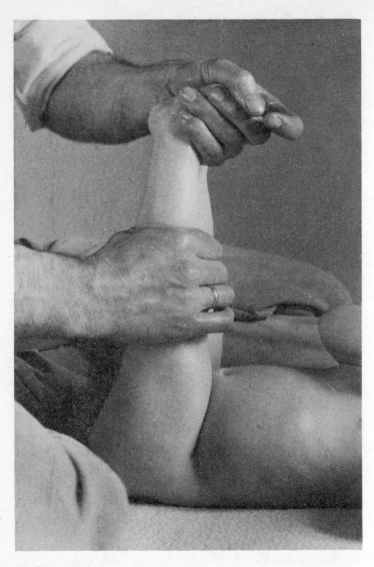

9. *"SWEDISH MILKING."* Milk the leg from ankle to hip.

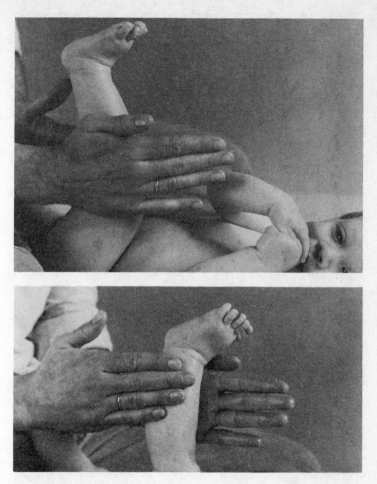

10. *"ROLLING."* Roll the leg between your hands from knee to ankle.

After massaging each leg and foot, massage the buttocks with both hands and stroke the legs to the feet, gently bouncing. This integrates both legs with the trunk and tells baby you are moving to another area.

# The Stomach

The strokes for the stomach will tone baby's intestinal system and help relieve gas and constipation. Most of the strokes end at baby's lower left belly (your right). This is where the eliminative part of the intestines is located. The purpose is to move gas and intestinal materials toward the bowel. Always stroke from the ribcage down, and use a clockwise motion for circular strokes.

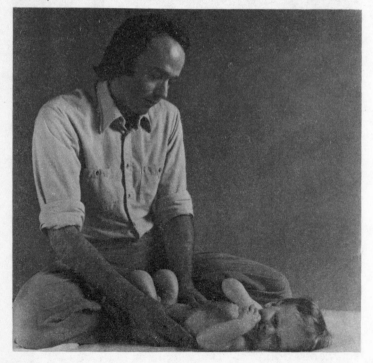

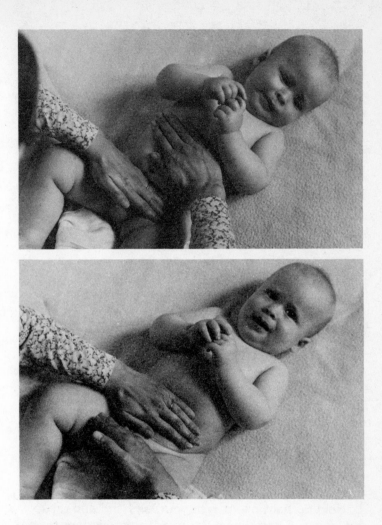

1. *"WATER WHEEL."*
a. Make paddling strokes on baby's tummy, one hand
following the other, as if you were scooping sand toward yourself.

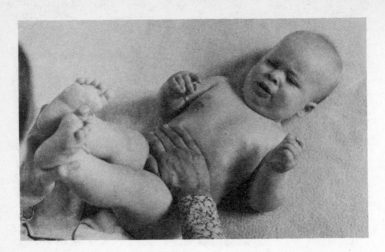

b. Hold up baby's legs with your left hand and grasp the ankles. Then repeat the paddling motion, using the right hand only. This will relax the stomach and will permit you to extend the massaging action a little more deeply.

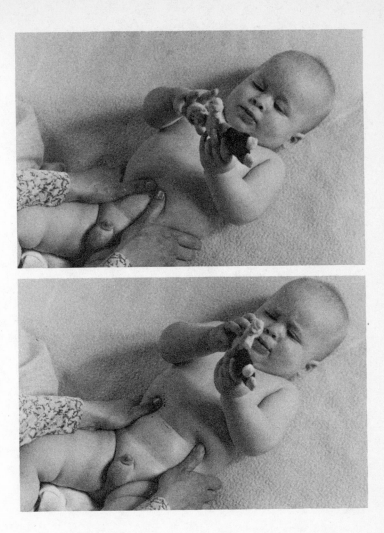

2. With thumbs flat at baby's navel, push out to the
sides. Be sure you use the flat thumb, and do not poke.

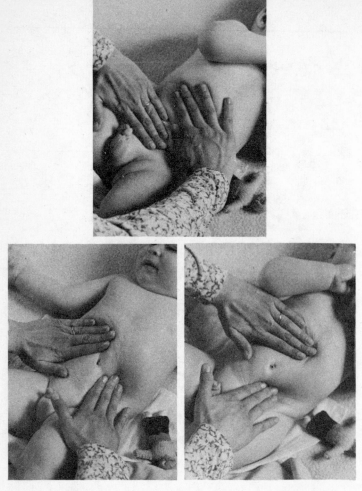

3. *"SUN MOON."* Your right hand makes an upside-down half-moon from your left to right. Your left hand makes a full circle, moving clockwise. While the right hand is above, the left hand is below.

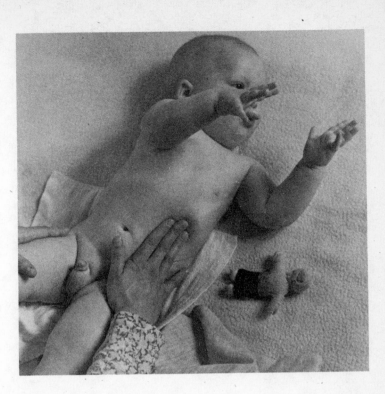

**4. "I LOVE YOU."**
a. Make a single *I*-shaped stroke with your right hand on baby's left belly (your right).

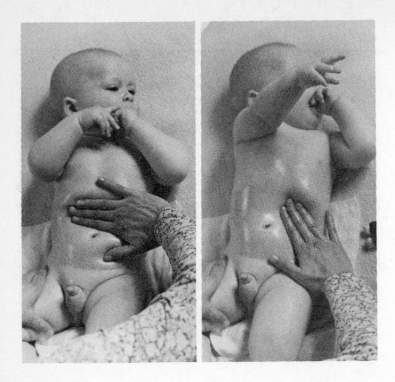

b. *"LOVE."* Make a backward, sideways *L* going from your left to right.

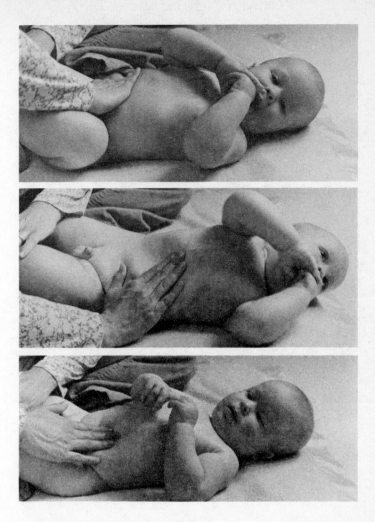

c. *"YOU."* Make an upside-down *U*, going from your left to right. As you go through this series of motions, say "I love you" in a high-pitched, cooing tone. Baby will love it!

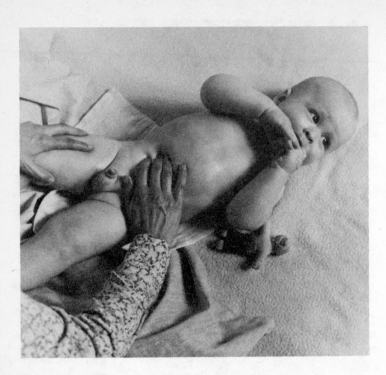

5. *"WALKING."* Using your fingertips, walk across baby's tummy from your left to right. You may feel some gas bubbles moving under your fingers.

# The Chest

Massaging the chest will help tone the lungs and the heart. Imagine that you are freeing the baby's breath, and filling his heart with love.

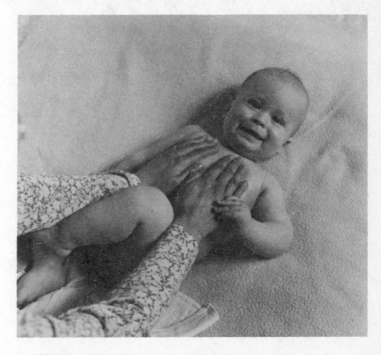

1. *"OPEN BOOK."* With both hands together at the center of the chest, push out to the sides, following the rib cage, as if you were flattening the pages of a book.

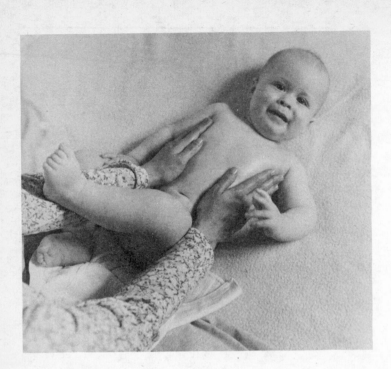

Without lifting the hands from the body, bring them around in a heart-shaped motion to center again.

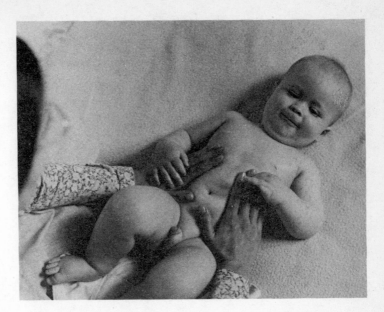

2. *"BUTTERFLY."*
a. To begin this movement, both hands are at the baby's sides, at the bottom of the rib cage.

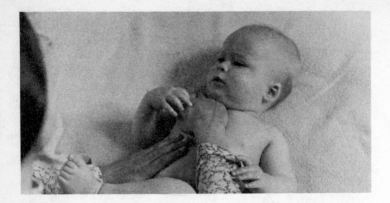

b. The right hand moves across the chest diagonally, to the baby's right shoulder; then, pulling gently at the shoulder, the hand moves down across the chest and back to its original position.

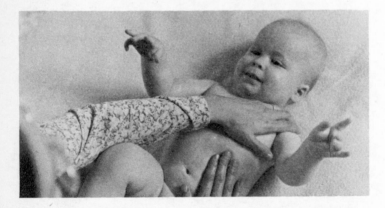

c. Now, the left hand moves across the chest diagonally, to the baby's left shoulder, repeating the same motion. Follow one hand with the other, rhythmically crisscrossing the chest.

# The Arms and Hands

When massaging the arms the complementary differences between Swedish and Indian methods are most strikingly revealed, especially in the "milking" motions.

The traditional Indian way is to "milk" the arm from shoulder to hand, imagining stress and tension leaving the body through the fingertips. The Swedish method is just the opposite, milking from the hand to the shoulder—toward the heart—for circulation. Using both methods, we combine the Indian concept of balancing and releasing energy with the muscle-toning Swedish massage.

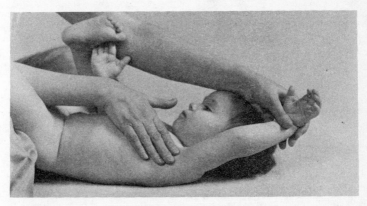

1. *"PIT STOP."* First stroke the armpit a few times, massaging the important lymph nodes in that area.

Some babies resist having their arms massaged, and will protectively hug their arms close to their chest. Rather than pulling outward on your baby's arm, massage it toward the direction she is holding it. Support her in protecting herself, massaging the arm in its "hug" position. When she begins to feel relaxed and supported, your baby will begin to relax her arms and "give" them to you to massage.

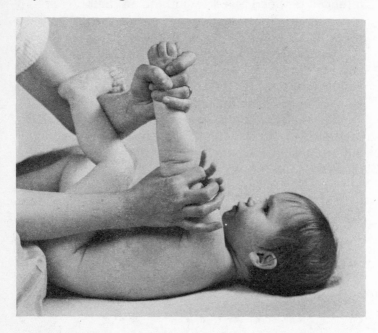

2. *"INDIAN MILKING."* Now, holding baby's wrist with your left hand, milk the arm with your right hand, starting at the shoulder and moving to the hand. Immediately follow with your left hand, then the right, and so forth. Use the inside edge of your hand, at the point where the thumb connects with the index finger.

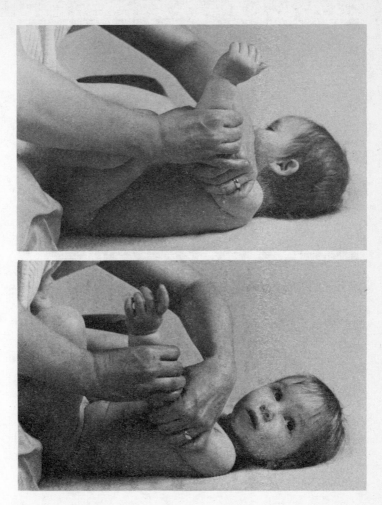

3. *"SQUEEZE AND TWIST."* Hold hands together around baby's arm at the shoulder (as if you were holding a baseball bat). Then move hands in opposite directions, back and forth, from the shoulder to the hand, gently squeezing as you do.

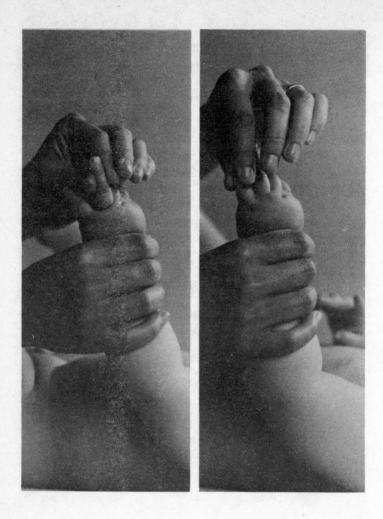

4. Open baby's hand with your thumbs. Roll each tiny finger between your index finger and thumb.

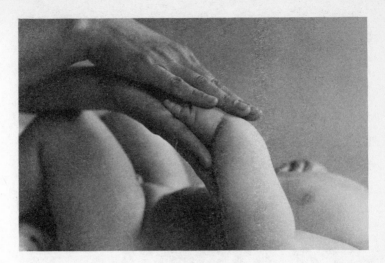

5. Stroke the top of the hand.

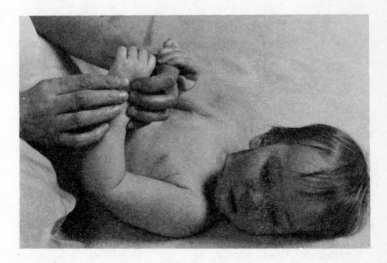

6. Massage the wrist, making small circles all around.

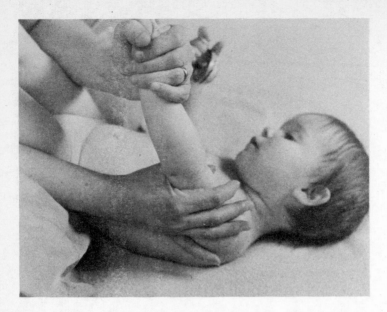

7. *"SWEDISH MILKING."* Milk the arm from the hand to the shoulder, with one hand following the other.

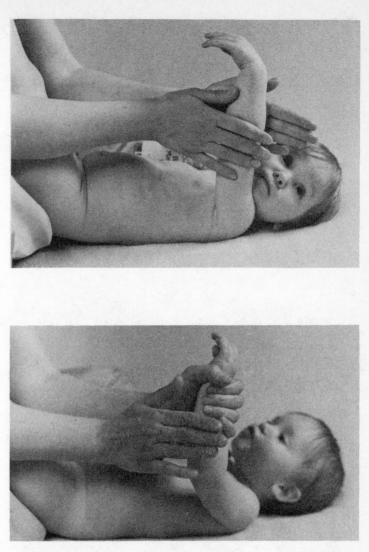

9. To help baby relax his arm, shake it gently and pat it lightly all over.

# The Face

Baby's face may accumulate a great deal of tension through sucking, teething, crying, and generally interacting with the ever-expanding world around him.

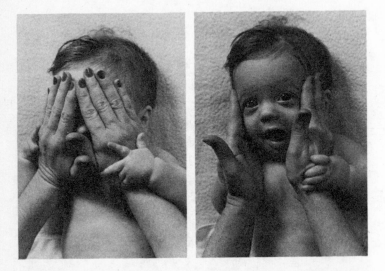

1. With the flats of the fingers, start at the middle of the forehead, and push out to the sides, as if flattening the pages of a book.

2. With the thumbs, press lightly over the eyes.

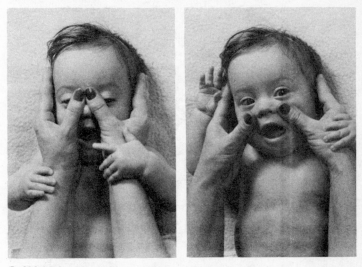

3. With the thumbs, push up on the bridge of the nose, then down across the cheeks.

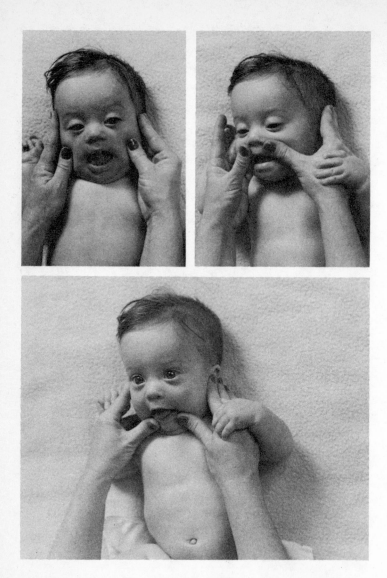

4. With the thumbs, make a smile on the upper, then the lower lip.

5. Make small circles around the jaw with your fingertips.

6. Using the fingertips of both hands, go over the ears, around the backs of the ears, and pull up under the chin. This helps relax the jaw and massages important lymph nodes in this area.

# The Back

The back is often a favorite with babies and toddlers alike. It is the most relaxing part of the massage. These strokes also act as a kind of warm-up for the exercises which follow.

To massage the back, turn baby on his tummy, either on the floor, or on your lap with your legs outstretched.

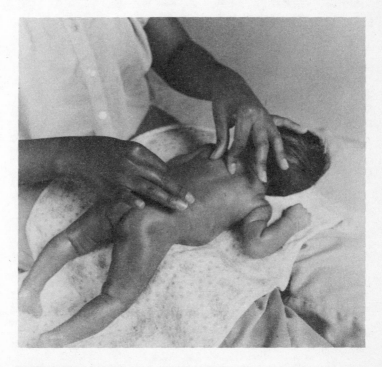

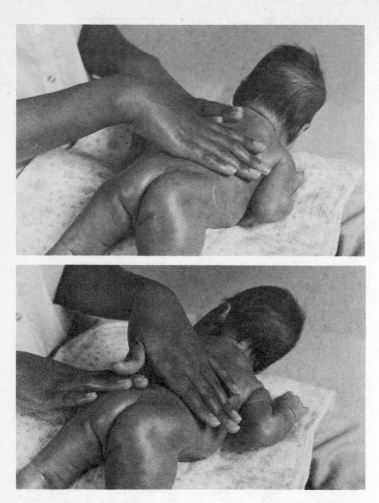

1. *"BACK AND FORTH."* Start with both hands together at the top of the back, at right angles to the spine. Move your hands back and forth, in opposite directions, going down the back to the buttocks, then up the shoulders, and back down once again.

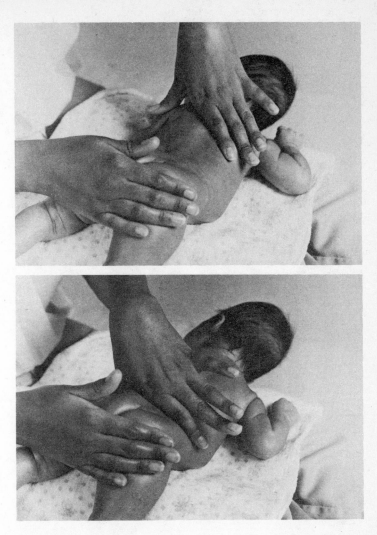

2. Keep the right hand stationary at the buttocks. Then, beginning at the neck, the left hand swoops down to meet the right hand at the buttocks.

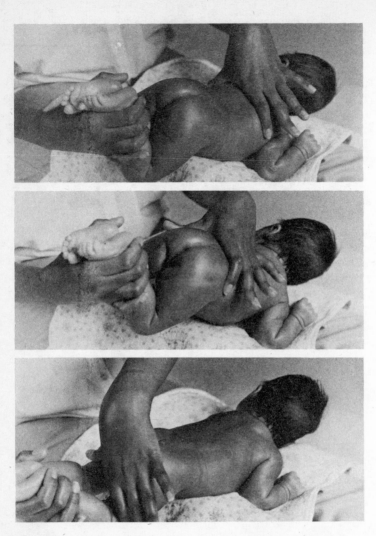

3. Hold up the legs with your right hand. Your left hand will then repeat the "swooping" motion, this time moving all the way down the legs to the ankles.

As baby grows, you can feel muscles develop right under your fingertips!

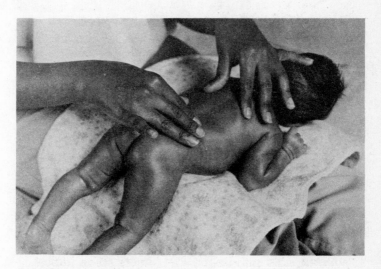

4. Make small circles all around the back with your fingertips.

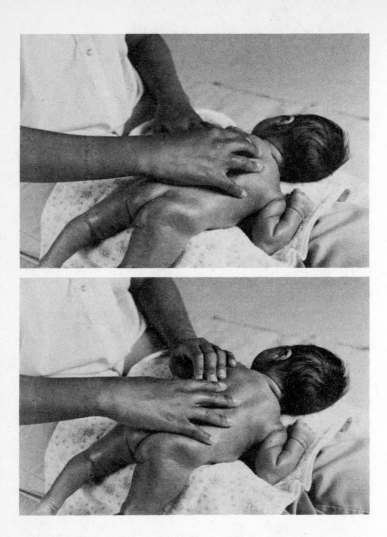

5. With the right hand open and fingers spread apart, the fingers "comb" the back, starting at the neck and moving to the buttocks. Each stroke will be progressively lighter, ending with a "feather touch."

# Gentle Movements

These movements are simple movements that gently stretch baby's arms and legs, massage his stomach and pelvis, and align his spine. Repeat four or five times.

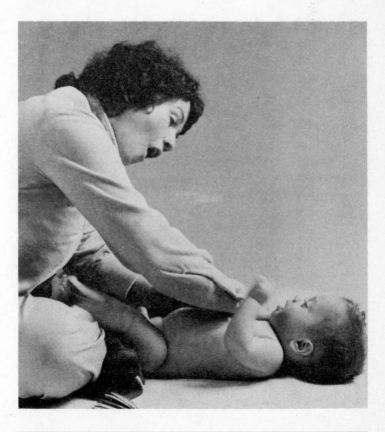

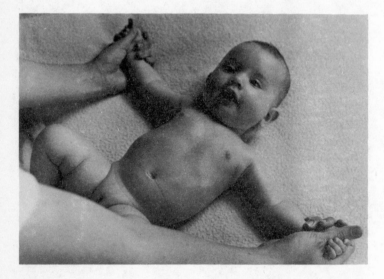

1. Holding baby's arms at the wrist, stretch them out to the sides, then cross them at his chest twice.

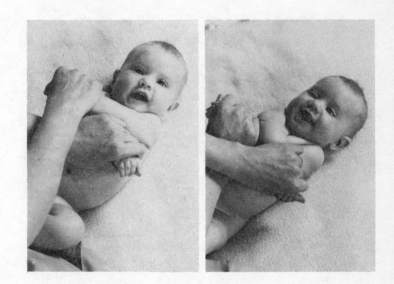

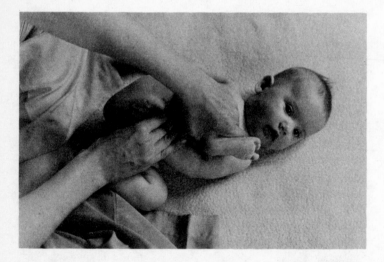

2. Hold one arm at the wrist, and the opposite leg at the
ankle. Gently bring the arm down to the crotch and the
foot up toward the shoulder, then cross the leg and arm
so that the arm goes to the outside of the leg. Now
stretch them out in opposite directions. Repeat with
opposite arm and leg. Note: With an older child, bring the
knee, rather than the foot, up to cross with the arm.

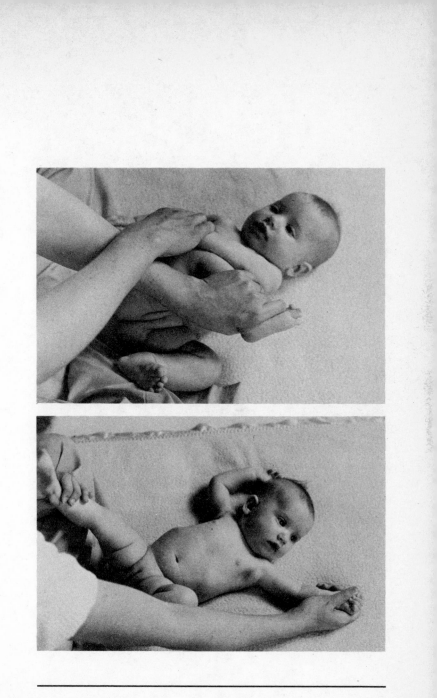

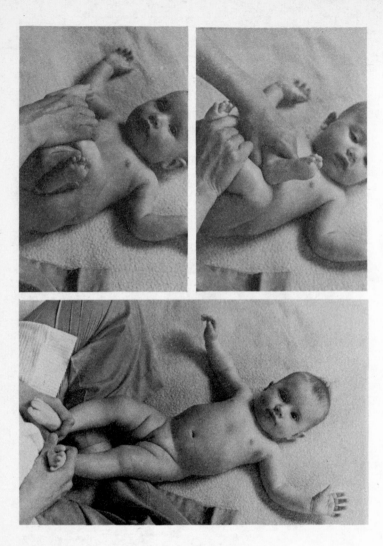

3. Holding the legs at the ankles
cross them at the stomach four times,
then stretch them out straight.

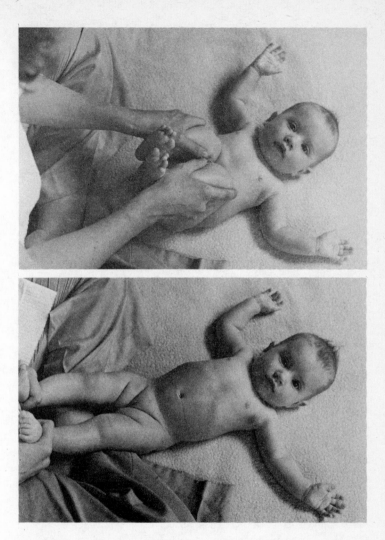

4. Push the knees together up into the tummy, then stretch them out straight. If baby resists straightening his legs, shake them gently and encourage him to relax.

# Review of
# the Strokes

1. Relax and breathe deeply as you remove baby's clothing.

2. Oil palms and rub together to warm.

3. Show palms to baby, ask permission to begin.

4. Legs and feet:
   a. Indian Milking
   b. Squeeze and Twist
   c. Thumb over thumb on sole of foot, toward toes
   d. Squeeze each toe
   e. Massage area adjacent to balls of foot
   f. Press in all over bottom of foot
   g. Massage over top of foot toward ankle
   h. Small circles around ankle
   i. Swedish Milking
   j. Rolling
   k. Massage both buttocks, stroking legs to feet

5. Stomach:
   a. Water Wheel
   b. Water Wheel with legs up
   c. Thumbs to sides
   d. Sun Moon
   e. I Love You
   f. Walking

6. Chest:

   a. Open Book
   b. Butterfly

7. Arms and Hands:

   a. Pit Stop
   b. Indian Milking
   c. Squeeze and Twist
   d. Open hand
   e. Roll each finger
   f. Top of hand
   g. Small circles around wrist
   h. Swedish Milking
   i. Rolling

8. Face:

   a. Open Book
   b. Thumbs over eyes
   c. Push up on bridge of nose, down across cheek
   d. Smile on upper and lower lip
   e. Small circles around jaw
   f. Over ears and under chin

9. Back:

   a. Back and Forth
   b. Swooping to bottom
   c. Swooping to ankles
   d. Small circles all over back
   e. Comb back

10. Gentle Movements:

    a. Cross arms
    b. Cross arm and leg
    c. Cross legs
    d. Legs up and down
    e. Legs up and down alternating

11. *And a Kiss to Grow On!*

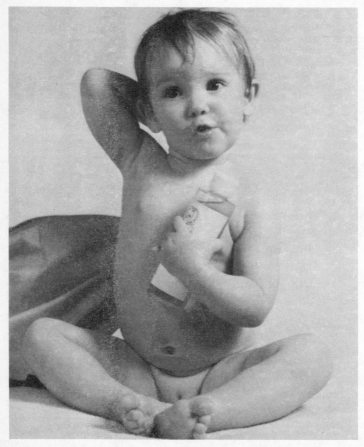

# ABBREVIATED MASSAGE

Sometimes you want to give baby a quick rub-down on the run, when changing diapers or just before bed. Here is an abbreviated massage that will take only a few minutes but will still provide the benefits of communication and relaxation your baby needs.

This massage can be done with or without oil or lotion.

1. Circles around head
2. Open Book on forehead
3. Circles on jaw
4. Open Book on chest
5. Roll arms, open hands
6. Sun Moon on stomach
7. Roll legs
8. Soles of feet
9. Back and Forth on back
10. Comb back

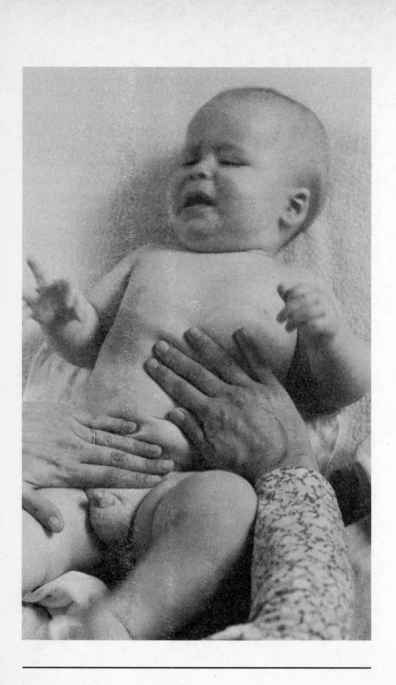

# CHAPTER NINE

# Infant
# Communication

This is my sad time of day.
—ARNOLD LOBEL

At this point you may be imagining yourself lovingly massaging your baby as he lies there contentedly listening to your voice, gazing into your eyes, and, perhaps, even falling asleep. This will probably happen quite often, and when it does it's wonderful. But it is also true that most babies will fuss or cry at times during their massage. If you understand the reasons for your baby's fussiness, you will be much more comfortable and better able to help him.

Infants grow so rapidly it is small wonder there is often so much tension in their little bodies. They are working so hard to develop muscle coordination that it is logical they may occasionally ache and feel out of sorts.

When your body aches, a massage feels both good and uncomfortable at the same time. Your muscles are sore and even a gentle touch can bring discomfort. Still, being touched is so relaxing, it's hard to tell if your grunts and grimaces are from pain or pleasure. Often a massage can remind you of aches you never knew you had, but afterward the feeling of relief and release you experience is well worth it.

Massage is a new experience for your little one. At first he may react negatively to the sensations he is experiencing, but after he becomes accustomed to being touched in this fashion he will begin to enjoy the routine. So take it easy at first and acquaint him with these new sensations slowly. Babies who have had difficult or traumatic births or who have had difficulties afterward for which they needed medical intervention tend to have more negative reactions to being massaged. For example, babies who have received routine heel-sticks for blood testing often cry hard when their feet are massaged, even several months later. Touch Relaxation is very effective with these areas. If your baby seems to be reacting in this way to particular parts of the massage, use Touch Relaxation techniques first, gradually introducing massage strokes as they are accepted.

## STAGES OF GROWTH

Babies commonly react to various massage strokes differently, according to their age and stage of development. Of course, every baby is unique and will not necessarily fit this picture; however, knowing common reactions can help you adjust the massage when you observe your own baby's behavior.

During the first three months, the baby displays many neonatal reflexes. The tonic neck reflex causes baby's head to turn to the side; the moro reflex can cause him to startle when unsupported. Massaging your baby in the "cradle pose" will help, because it offers warmth and support and keeps his head aligned. Many infants hold their arms in tight, with fists closed, and become anxious when their arms are massaged. If this is extreme, use Touch Relaxation to help the baby relax and release this tension before beginning to introduce the massage strokes. Observing your baby closely, you will see how hard he is working to strengthen and coordinate his arms. Because he has held them near his body for months in the womb, having them pulled on may be a downright scary feeling. Show him that it is okay to open and relax his arms. Touch his arms in a gentle and loving fashion, and stroke with, rather than against, the way he is naturally holding them. He will probably enjoy the strokes for the legs and the back during this period, and this feeling will, in turn, help him to relax his arms.

During the second three months of life most babies begin to look around their environment and they enjoy interacting with people. Tension can be found in the back because the baby is exercising these muscles in preparation for crawling and standing. The face can also hold tension from crying, teething, sucking, and interacting so intensely with people. At this stage many babies particularly enjoy having their stomachs, chests, and arms massaged. Your baby will begin to learn how to roll over during this stage; if so, let him do so during the massage and simply adjust the massage routine, stroking the back and legs.

Mobility is a major focus for seven- to twelve-month-old babies. Massage is a challenge because the baby is so intent upon moving about that it is no longer the relaxing experience it used to be. You can continue inventing strokes that are useful as your baby moves around.

Toward the end of the first year, tension may move into the legs as baby learns to stand and walk. This can be an especially trying time for some babies, who will steadfastly refuse to be massaged at all. Every bit of their attention will be focused on walking and teething. They may be very fussy and short-tempered until they have mastered the art of walking and have most of their teeth. Then they will slow down a little, having accomplished gargantuan feats during their first year of life. In Chapter Thirteen we'll go into further detail about changing the massage routine as your baby grows older.

## FUSSING

Some babies need time to become accustomed to being massaged, and will, at first, become fussy after just a few minutes. Breathe deeply and make every effort to relax. Then allow the baby to fuss a little. Often he will release the tension during the massage and be a lot happier, more relaxed, and sleep more soundly the rest of the time. The fussing will diminish as tension is released and the baby's stimulation threshold rises.

If your baby consistently begins to fuss at a certain point in the massage, it may be that he needs a break or a shorter massage period for a while. You can take a break to nurse or cuddle, then try again. If he continues to fuss, you may try massaging for a shorter period next time, at a different time of day, starting on a different area of his body the following day. Check to be sure he is warm enough and that you are relaxed and comfortable. Listen closely to what he is saying "under" the fussing; perhaps he needs to tell you about his day! Check for gas or colic (Chapter Ten) and listen, listen, listen. Your baby has a lot to say and needs to be heard.

## CRYING

Once, on a television news spot, I was asked to demonstrate infant massage and talk about its benefits. As we hurried to the studio, the host said, "I hear you have a way to stop a baby's screams in ten seconds flat with massage. I hope you can show us that today!"

The baby, a sweet four-month-old with whom I'd had a lovely conversation in the waiting room, took one look at the newscaster and began to cry inconsolably. I did not demonstrate massage because I felt it would betray her feelings to use it as a trick to quiet her (even if it could have, which I doubt). The host concluded that the infant massage gimmick did not work. She was right. As a gimmick, it does not. Unfortunately, many people think that babies should be seen and not heard.

As babies, we had few ways beyond crying to express negative feelings and release pent-up stress. Growing up, we learned how to deal with anger, fear, pain, and excess energy in many ways; facial expressions, body language, and speech patterns now help us to convey how we feel. When the stresses of living pile up, we can go for a walk, take a vacation, or talk to a friend. Even when we are healthy we cry from time to time, but rarely in front of others. We have learned that crying is antisocial and a sign of weakness. This was probably one of our earliest lessons.

The idea of "spoiling" came into vogue in the early part of this century. People began to think that they should let babies "cry it out" alone. The rationale was that babies used crying to manipulate parents into gratifying babies' desires, and that this was an unattractive character trait. Responding to it could only cultivate spoiled, boorish children leading their parents around by the nose. In order to teach babies that crying was unacceptable behavior and to train them for independence early, they were left alone to cry until they grew hoarse and fell asleep from sheer exhaustion.

In the 1970s a movement away from these earlier infant-rearing practices gained momentum. Many more women began breastfeeding, the front and back packs were invented, and baby experts began encouraging parents to interact more closely with their infants. Research told us that babies who are responded to cry less, not more, and that they are more, rather than less independent later on. Other cultures influenced this change; global communications had become sophisticated enough for us to begin looking more closely at cultures on the other side of the world which had not yet been impaired by so-called modern thinking.

Unfortunately, we had. Mothers who previously might have left baby alone to cry while they felt guilty and tearful in the adjacent room now jumped at the baby's smallest peep. But something remained. Getting the baby to stop crying, or not allowing the baby to cry at all, was still our obsession.

There are times when we need to cry. It is a release, and crying in the loving arms of another is often much more so. I believe that babies' feelings are as deep as ours, that their fears, their sorrows, and their frustrations are no less. From observing hundreds of babies in massage classes and in other cultures, I know that sometimes crying can be a relief and a release for infants.

Many of us brought up in the age of "don't spoil the baby" have mixed feelings about crying. We get anxious, tense up, and want the crying to stop right away. It triggers fear and perhaps a reminder of the anguish (and anger) we may have felt crying alone in a crib with no response. It can also engender guilt—am I a bad mother if my baby cries?

Our culture often reinforces these feelings. Many people are extremely agitated by any noise a baby makes and assail his parent with dour looks at the slightest sound. The embarrassed parent often responds by punishing the baby with loud hisses, apologizing for the baby, and fleeing for the safety of home. Because of a lack of social support, the demands of our economy, and social values which do not encourage family bonding, most new parents in western cultures periodically experience extremely high levels of stress, regardless of their parenting philosophies. Who has not had thoughts of "throwing the baby out the window" or fears of losing control and shaking or yelling

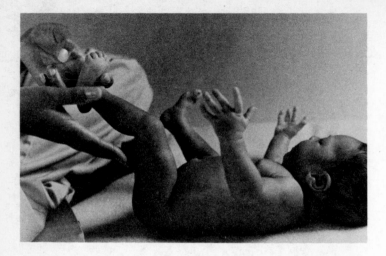

at a crying baby?

Like all of us, babies have many different reasons for crying. Unfortunately, we have lost much of our capacity to intuit their thoughts and feelings. Most people are able to recognize a sharp cry of pain, but our interpretation of other cries and fusses are filtered through the veil of our own insecurities and projections. It may be easier to adopt a mechanistic philosophy whereby we always respond in the same way—either ignoring or hushing. But babies are not interested in philosophy and are unable to attend to their parents' comfort. They need the response of clear thinking, caring, centered adults to help them find a way through this world of unknowns. Daily massage can help you intuitively understand your baby's vocalizations because it helps you to literally keep in touch with your baby's body language and nonverbal signals.

Actively and compassionately listening to an infant isn't much different from listening to a child or adult. It requires empathy, genuine love, and respect for the infant's experience. I believe that the reason it is so difficult for us to listen to our babies is that our own infancies may have been full of frustration and unheard feelings. When we hear our babies cry, rather than truly listening to what they say, we superimpose our own inner infant. Our overwhelming impulse is to quiet *that* baby.

## HOW TO LISTEN TO A BABY

You can use a three-step process when your baby begins to vocalize, fuss, or cry during massage. First, take a long, slow, deep breath and relax your whole body. This directly counteracts the tendency to hold your breath and tighten up.

Second, set aside your own inner infant for a moment, recognizing that, in order to truly hear your baby, you must clear yourself. Third, make eye contact with the baby if possible. If your baby is avoiding eye contact, place your hands gently but firmly on his body and connect with him through your hands. Let your love go to him, telling him with your voice, your eyes, and your hands that you would like to hear what he has to say.

Stay with the baby, keeping yourself very relaxed and receptive. Listen and respond to him, observing his body language. Watch his mouth and what he says

with his eyes. When you are sure that he feels heard and has said most of what he has to say, offer the comfort of rocking, walking, and cuddling to help him get organized again. Invariably, a baby who feels "heard" will sleep more deeply afterward and will extend himself in trust more the next time.

When we truly listen to our infants we are fulfilling all of their psychological needs. The underlying message is, "You are worthy of respect. You are valuable just the way you are." The baby takes in this message, and his whole body relaxes. The chalice of this infant's heart is filled to overflowing, and as he grows he will seek opportunities to share his love with others. How will he do this? By following the model he has been given. He will be there for others in the way you have been there for him. What a lovely, healthy cycle!

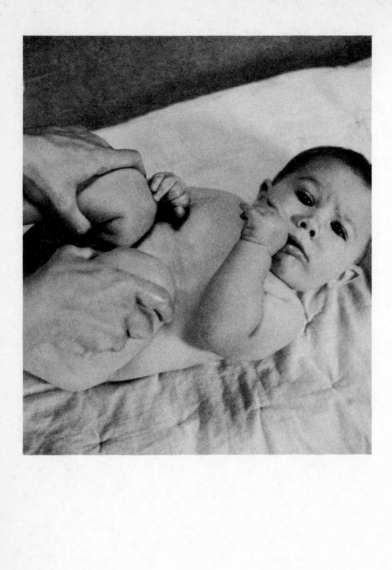

# CHAPTER TEN

# Illness and Colic

Can a mother sit and hear
An infant groan, an infant fear?
No, no! Never can it be!
Never, never can it be!
—WILLIAM BLAKE

In times of illness a massage not only can be comforting but can also help relieve such painful symptoms as aches, fever, and congestion. Of course, as is the case with any significant deviation from health in your baby, consult your family doctor about its use.

To help bring down a fever you may use some of the same strokes as in the basic massage. Use warm water on your hands instead of oil, and keep baby's body covered, except the part you're working on. Working from the chest to the extremities, dip your hand in the water, then briskly rub the body. The idea is to bring the heat up to the surface of the skin, where the water will evaporate and help cool it.

You can use a similar technique with your baby to help ease chest congestion. First, do the regular massage motions for the chest, using oil on your hands. (A little eucalyptus or Mentholatum may also help.) Then, tip the baby at an angle with his head down. Using a small cup (the clean plastic cap from a bottle of fabric softener works nicely) or something with a small rim, press in and pull out gently all over the chest and back. The gentle suction helps pull mucus away from the lungs so it can be coughed up. A vaporizer in baby's room will help, too.

For nasal congestion, assemble the following: a nasal aspirator, a dropper, a handkerchief, and a cup of warm salted water (ratio: ½ tsp. salt per cup of warm water). Do the massage motions for the face, especially the ones for the sinus area, to help relax the area and loosen mucus. Then place a drop of the warm salted water in each nostril, and suction out the mucus with the aspirator, blowing it into the handkerchief after each time. The warm salt water is easy on baby's nose and helps loosen the mucus considerably. Baby will not enjoy this process, but it may be necessary if his stuffiness is preventing him from being able to suck.

## GAS AND COLIC

Babies often cry because of painful gas or because they are tired and disorganized. It is very common for babies to experience discomfort and outright pain from trapped gas. Their gastrointestinal systems need prompting to begin to function the way they should, and massage can provide just the right type of stimulation.

There has been much speculation over the years concerning colic and its causes. The label "colic" is often used for any baby who cries often; I prefer to use it for babies who cry for extended periods of time and are obviously experiencing pain. In addition, a truly colicky baby will be stiff and tense, have a distended abdomen, and have difficulty tolerating stimulation. A baby with discomfort from gas that is not so severe cries often, pulls his legs up and seems to be in pain, and may expel gas in short bursts. Often the gassy baby can be comforted by walking or rhythmic rocking and holding, while the colicky baby may or may not be comforted during an episode.

Massage can help any baby—from mildly gassy to extremely colicky. It stimulates the gastrointestinal system to do its job, it helps release built-up stress, and the Touch Relaxation techniques help the baby learn to relax.

## A COLIC-RELIEF ROUTINE

First of all, of course, try to relax yourself. A gassy or colicky baby is a challenge for any parent, and your stress overload can make you feel edgy and confused. Remember, you are not at fault for your baby's discomfort, but you can help him. Listen to his cries with respect for his feelings, and then get to work to help him manage his episodes.

Massage the baby twice a day for two weeks, using the techniques given below. Count the strokes and hold the knees-up position, then help baby relax with Touch Relaxation, using your voice, your hands, and rhythmic patting or light bouncing to help him loosen up. Here's the routine:

1. Do the Water Wheel stroke six times, one hand following the other.

---

2. Hold baby's knees together, then push up into his tummy, holding for about a half minute (see photograph, page 117).

3. Gently release pressure, stroke his legs, and use Touch Relaxation to coax him to release them.

4. Do the Sun Moon stroke six times, one hand following the other.

5. Hold baby's knees together, then push up into his tummy, holding for about a half minute.

6. Gently release pressure, stroke his legs, and use Touch Relaxation to coax him to release them.

Repeat this entire cycle three times. It may take several days before the baby responds; often a baby will begin expelling gas on the first try. His system will begin to function more and more smoothly, so that whenever he has an episode, a short massage will help break up and release trapped gas. Not every baby responds in the same way, and some, because of other factors, will not benefit as much as others. Many pediatricians now refer parents of gassy or colicky babies to infant massage as a way to address the problem without drugs. Penny, mother of three-week-old Matthew, was nearly at the end of her rope with his colic; her pediatrician recommended that she try massage, so she contacted me. "Matthew was very colicky until two weeks after I began massaging him, at which point the episodes began to subside," she says. "Within a few weeks his colic disappeared completely. Now his disposition is very pleasant. He trusts me and I have become much more relaxed." When I first met Penny and Matthew, they were each so stressed by the colic that they had difficulty interacting with each other at all. Within two weeks, the change was remarkable. They were looking at each other, playing together, and Matthew was beginning to really enjoy the massage. Even when she did the colic-relief routine, Matthew seemed to cooperate and "work with it." He would wiggle and grunt and expel gas with each round of strokes, and responded well to the Touch Relaxation techniques.

Other aids included warm baths, glycerin suppositories, and changes in diet. If you are nursing, check your diet for irritants such as tomatoes, chocolate, caffeine, and gas-producing beans and vegetables. Sometimes a milk or wheat allergy can cause colic; try eliminating one or both and see if there is any change in baby's discomfort.

It isn't easy to see your little one in such distress, and it can be terribly draining both physically and emotionally. "Being able to massage my baby and help him relax gave me peace of mind," says Mary, mother of eighteen-month-old Michael. "I started massaging him when he was two weeks old and having painful gassy spells, and I saw results within a week. When he woke up crying in the middle of the night, I would massage him. After only a week, he'd begin to relax as soon as I started stroking him. He'd calm down and start releasing; often, he fell asleep before I finished. I felt so good, being able to do something to help him, not to mention the extra hours of sleep it gave me! Even now, when he gets tense and out-of-sorts, I can talk to him and stroke him a little, and he relaxes. I wouldn't have known what to do for him otherwise; his infancy could have been just a disaster for all of us."

Because of the incredible stress of having a colicky baby, it is natural to feel somewhat negative and discouraged. Massage can be a way to help your baby and thus boost your feelings of confidence and your self-esteem; it's worth a try.

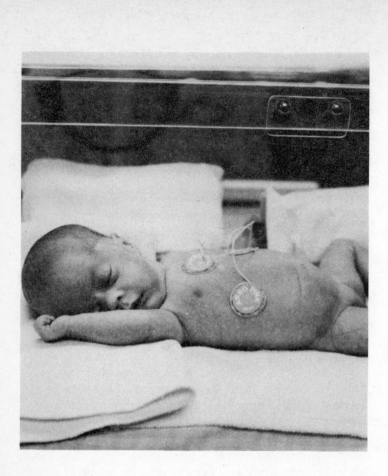

# CHAPTER ELEVEN

# The Premature Baby

Mother, let us imagine we are travelling,
and passing through a strange
and dangerous country.

—TAGORE

We know how important it is to hold our babies
close, right from the start. A lot of planning
goes into those first few hours and weeks as
we arrange to avoid the interruptions that would un-
necessarily deprive our babies of those precious moments of bonding time.

When a baby arrives into the world long before she
is expected, the best-laid plans are obliterated. The
quiet, warm, joyous welcome hoped for is abruptly re-
placed by a kind of violence we never imagined. It is
an unavoidable violence, one that keeps the baby alive,
but also one that engenders a tremendous range of
feelings and reactions in parents.

Parents are thrust into cycles of grief: shock, denial (often manifesting as an obsession with the baby's medical condition as opposed to his recovery), guilt ("What did I do to cause this?"), anger (at baby, at spouse, at medical people, at fate), depression (often creating distance between parents and their baby), bargaining ("I'll be the best parent ever if he just pulls through"), and fear. These feelings and many variations of them are natural and may recur in cycles for a long time after the baby's birth. Parents recover from the initial shock at different rates; most finally do accept the situation and begin trying to find ways to help their baby through it and initiate the bonding process.

What about the baby? Thrust into cycles of her own—shock, pain, fear, withdrawal—the premature baby may be ignored as an emotional, feeling human being while the adults around her focus on lifesaving. This kind of treatment sometimes extends far beyond what is necessary, objectifying the baby and pushing an emotional wedge between the child and her parents—between the child and the world.

The preemie's first contact with human touch brings pain: needles, probes, tubes, rough handling, bright lights—all sudden, after the warm protection of the womb. One of the first things parents can do to help and to begin bonding is to massage their baby. It is a wonderful expression of caring that contributes to both physical and psychological healing, not only for babies but for parents, too. Much of the anguish of those first days and weeks can be minimized if parents can feel some sense of control.

Many studies have proven that premature babies who are regularly stroked and who regularly hear their parents' voices during their nursery stay improve rap-

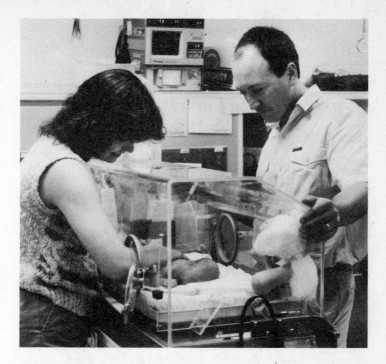

idly in growth and development. Judith Talaba, head nurse in a neonatal intensive care unit, has introduced massage as a regular part of every baby's routine. "Massage gives parents a focus on the baby as an individual who needs her parents just as much as she needs the technology," she says. "Parents in our nursery have become less concerned with oxygen concentrations, weight gain, and intake amounts, and more concerned about their infants being touched and massaged—a wonderful change of focus." She adds that preemies in the intensive care unit have responded positively to massage, losing hyperflexia (contraction of the body) and "withdrawing-from-touch" behaviors.

Many have also had fewer apnea (cessation of breathing) spells.

## MASSAGING YOUR PREMATURE BABY IN THE HOSPITAL

Preemies love the feeling of enclosure that a pair of warm, loving hands can give. But it is important to go very slowly, very tenderly. Before beginning a regular routine of massage (I recommend at least once daily), look around your baby's environment. What changes might be made to help the baby relax and feel more comfortable, less invaded? Sometimes small changes in light, sound, and handling can make a big difference.

A certain amount of light is necessary for the nurses to be able to observe the baby, but most nurseries will allow you to shade the baby's sensitive eyes. If your child is on a "warming table," you can shield the head with an overturned box (such as a diaper box) with holes cut in all sides. In an incubator, a folded towel on top will do the trick. When the baby has stabilized, you can request that the incubator be shaded at night to help your child regulate to cycles of day and night.

For a stark example of how we objectify our infants, observe an adult intensive care unit and then a neonatal intensive care unit. Often the babies are subjected to loud conversation, ringing telephones, and rock music; the adult area is calm and quiet. Additional noise that we may not notice includes the high decibels of incubator motors, the clatter of instruments and clipboards, the slamming of the incubator door. You can request nursery staff to lower the tone of conversation and music. You can fasten a sign on the incubator requesting gentle closing, and place a towel on top to dampen the clang of instruments.

Sounds that help your baby feel more comfortable can be introduced. Premature babies, like all babies, are soothed by their mother's voice and heartbeat sounds. When you are unable to be present, a recording of your voice might be played at intervals. First check it out with the baby; be sure the volume is low and not distressing. When you are there, talk and sing to your baby. Even if your child doesn't seem to respond, she is listening. Your baby remembers your voice, and it soothes her.

Your little one's first reactions to handling may be distressing. Go slowly: watch, listen, and learn from

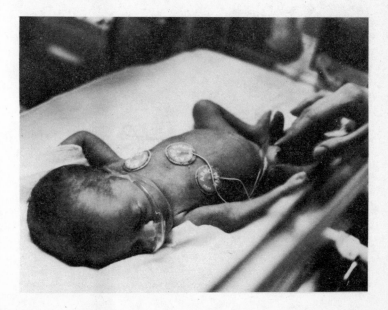

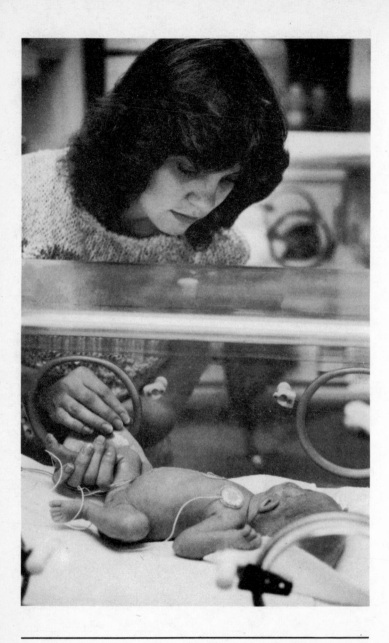

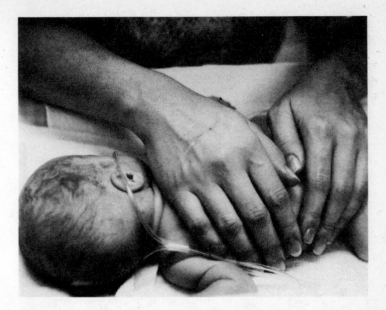

your baby. A preemie's distress signals, which include apnea and bradycardia (reduced heart rate), can instill so great a fear that you may find yourself making excuses not to handle her.

In actuality, and not surprisingly, studies have shown that mothers are best able to reduce their preemie's distress. Breathe deeply, relax, and move through these moments with your baby. Assure your newborn that she is okay, that you are here to love and care for her no matter what happens. The baby needs to feel your strength and confidence.

Observe your infant's alertness cycles to find when the best time may be for massage. Discover what kinds of stimulation she can handle. Some babies are extremely sensitive and can cope with only one modality at a time—touching, or talking, or eye contact, but

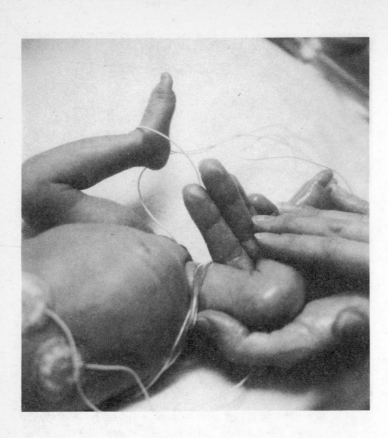

not all three at once. Find out what kinds of drugs
your baby has been given. Some (such as curare and
pavulon) will make the baby unresponsive. Even then,
your baby is aware of you, can feel and hear you, and
needs your loving touch.

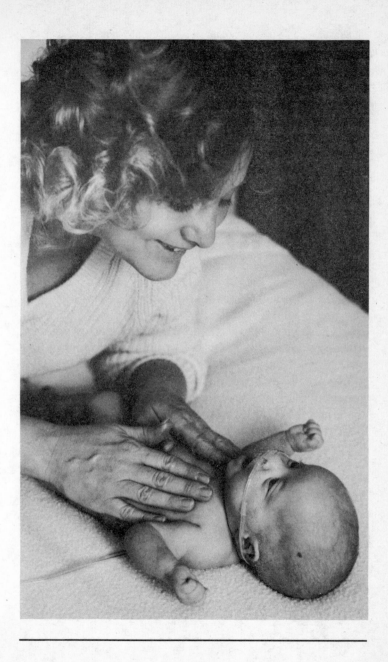

# HOW TO BEGIN

You should be able to begin massaging your baby when she reaches around 1000 grams in weight. When you have prepared and feel a little more comfortable handling her, you can begin a regular routine. It is as simple as holding your baby's tiny body in cupped hands, with a feeling of deep relaxation. In the beginning you need not be concerned about how to do certain strokes. Just hold each part of the baby's body for a few moments. Breathe deeply, feel relaxation and warmth in your hands. Using some light, natural oil or lotion, slowly and gently rub the baby's skin all over, working around the tubes, gauze, and other items that may be attached. Respect your baby's communication, however subtle it may be.

Conveying respect is an important part of infant massage. While the baby is forming initial feelings about herself and her body, whatever you reflect back to her will be taken seriously. This does not mean that you must abruptly stop the massage if the baby gives a signal that you interpret as negative. You want to help your child work through her fears, not reinforce them.

For example, babies who keep their arms tightly held to their chests are indicating a need to protect this area of the body. Rather than pry the arms apart, stroke them in the direction of their contraction. This tells the child, "I support your need to protect yourself. I'm on your side." Of course, you do want to watch for signs that the baby has had enough and not go beyond what she can accept.

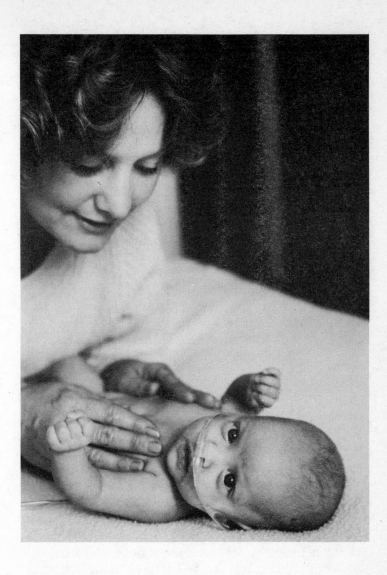

# EYE CONTACT

A powerful connection is made when your baby first looks into your eyes. Eye contact is one of the important components in the dance of bonding, and one of the joys of massage. But preemies, because they are not yet ready to regulate themselves, need your help. Your baby may avoid eye contact altogether. You can gently offer encouragement by reducing harsh lights and positioning the baby so that you are accessible. Or, your baby may become "locked in"—unable to release herself from looking and eventually becoming overstressed. If this happens, you can gently unlock baby's gaze after a moment or two by moving aside, passing a hand in front of his face, or shifting the baby's position.

As your baby grows, the ability to communicate with you through eye contact will grow. Be patient, and don't force it. With slow and steady encouragement, you will soon treasure this important part of your bond.

# TROUBLE SPOTS

Premature babies' bodies have been traumatized. Observe which areas of your baby's body may be especially programmed for pain. Usually the feet, head, and chest are quite sensitive. At first, you may not be able to get to some of these areas because of the equipment. When you can reach them, begin like this:

1. Hold the baby's foot (head, chest, etc.) in your

hands as if you are cupping a precious gem between your palms.

2. Deeply relax all over. Let this deep relaxation course from your heart, through your arms and hands, to your baby.

3. Talk to the baby about relaxing her feet. Acknowledge that she has had a lot of pain in this area, and that she has been very courageous. You are here to help her release the pain and let pleasure in. Let your baby know that soon this painful time will be over, and she will be healthy and happy, ready to do what she wants to do in life. Use some key word or phrase such as "relax" or "let go" as you gently rock the area back and forth.

4. When the baby responds with relaxation, praise her effort.

Repeat these steps every day, if possible, until you feel that the baby may be ready for more. Then you can begin gently massaging the area with oil, using the same relaxation and affirmation throughout.

## MASSAGING YOUR BABY AT HOME

You can really begin to work with your baby when she comes home from the hospital. Keep in mind that it is quite a change for the baby, and that she may regress a little. You may have to back up a bit with the massage, again focusing on relaxation and release.

In the warmth and security of your home environment, your baby will at last be able to release the tension and trauma of the hospital stay. This can be frightening and difficult for parents; suddenly the baby may be crying all the time. You may feel a little insecure without the hospital staff, as much as you might have resented their intrusions. At a time when you need reassurance, your baby's feedback seems to be, "I don't like it here!"

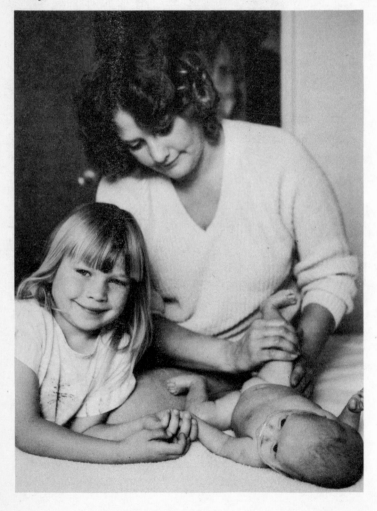

Actually, the intense crying, if not caused by pain, is a healthy release. Often a baby will cry especially hard after the massage. This does not mean that your child dislikes it or that you are doing it incorrectly. This is simply the only way available for the baby to release all the pent-up anguish. You can support your child by trying to relax and allow her to do what she needs to do, by being there to lovingly comfort her, and by trying to release your own fears. If you feel like crying with the baby (who wouldn't?), go right ahead.

Eventually you will progress from simple relaxation and holding to massage. Still, you must account for the differences between massaging your baby and massaging a full term infant. Begin with the place on the baby's body which has been least invaded—usually this is the back. Miniaturize every stroke. You can follow the strokes in Chapter Eight and simply modify them; for example, use two or three fingers instead of the whole hand. But do not be afraid to be firm. Your baby loves to feel the strength of your presence; a feathery touch can be overstimulating and annoying.

Be sure the space is very warm and that the baby is enclosed (use cradle pose) and near you. You may want to warm the oil beforehand, but swishing it between your hands should be sufficient. Soon you will find that just the sound of the oil between your palms will cause your baby to open like a little flower. With your help, she will learn to anticipate being massaged as a pleasurable experience, a time to feel the security of your loving hands. Once the tension is out of the body, your baby's system will regulate. You will find marked improvement in her sleeping, feeding, digestion, and elimination, and you will notice a decrease in crying. Watch your baby bloom open to acceptance of life.

If possible, schedule yourself for an all-body massage by a competent, licensed therapist. You, too, have been through quite an ordeal. If you can release your own tensions and trauma, your baby will respond more positively to your touch.

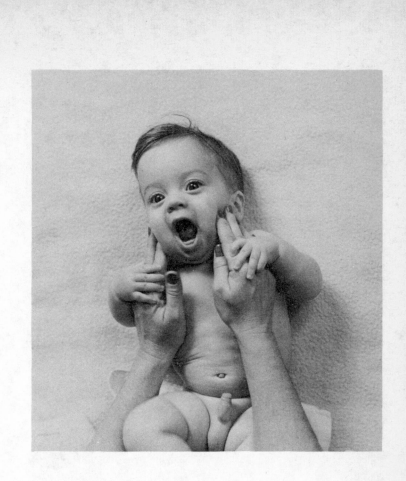

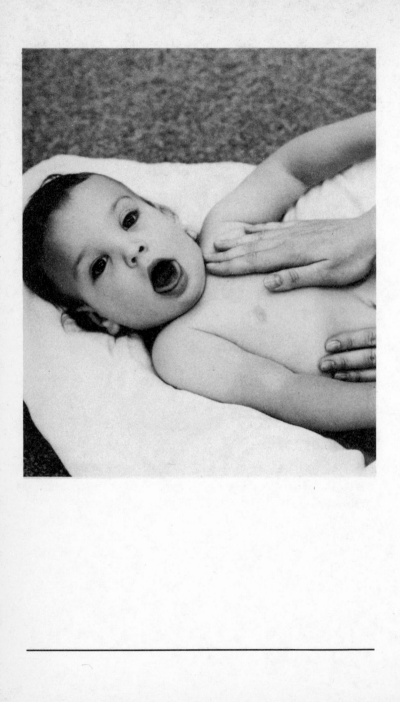

# CHAPTER TWELVE

# Massaging the Baby With Special Needs

*The most important thing to remember
is that these kids are more normal than they are
abnormal. Your child (no matter what kind of handicap
he has) is more like other children than unlike them.*
                              —MELISSA SURGUINE-SMITH
                                  from *After the Tears*

B onding is a matter of reciprocal interaction; it is dependent upon a parent stimulating the infant with appropriate cues or signals, which trigger a response in the infant. The infant's cues or signals then trigger further involvement by the parent, including eye contact, smiling, speech sounds, and body movements. The baby with mental, visual, hearing, or developmental impairments sometimes cannot respond in the "normal" manner to parental cues. Interactional synchrony is thus sometimes inhibited and can lead to the parent feeling out of touch with her baby. In addition, parents of babies with impairments are often overwhelmed by all of the information they need to absorb, by the therapies they are expected to carry out, and by the double bind of grieving and bonding at the same time.

Parents' emotional reactions to the discovery of an impairment in their newborn differ greatly. They can include confusion, denial, guilt, anger, wishful thinking, depression, intellectualization, and acceptance. These natural feelings can overlap and recur as parent and child adjust to their life together and to each new stage of the baby's development.

Infant massage can be a wonderful bonding tool for parents and babies with special needs. While physiological benefits accrue, it is the interaction and connection of these two people that is the focus and goal of infant massage. It is something you do *with* your baby rather than *to* your baby. Infant massage is not another therapy; rather, it is an opportunity to share your love. A daily massage connects parent and baby in a way which is unmatched by any other type of interaction. Babies with special needs benefit from this intimacy even more than other babies. Because some avenues of communication may not be open to them, it is important that their parents know them well; the way the body feels when tense or relaxed, the look and feel of the abdomen when gassy or not, the difference between pain and tension. Often parents need to be acutely aware of their infants' bodies because life-threatening infections can arise. A parent who is attuned to the look and feel of her baby's body at all times will often be able to detect toxicity in the early stages.

Elizabeth has cystic fibrosis, and her mother is glad she learned infant massage when Elizabeth was an infant. "At first we didn't massage our baby every day," she says, "but the more we did it and saw how wonderfully she responded, it grew on us. Elizabeth doesn't have her problem with being cold any more (if she does, we give her a massage). She does not have so much abdominal pain, and her whole body is relaxed. Now when we massage Elizabeth we don't concentrate so much on cystic fibrosis, but on Elizabeth as a beautiful little human being, a person. Infant massage has helped us have a relationship with her that has gone beyond our expectations ... it gives us great hope; we are thankful for and enjoying our Elizabeth."

In the following sections, we will be discussing particular challenges and how the massage may be altered for various types of impairments. Before beginning a massage routine with your baby, check with his or her doctor and physical therapist; they will be able to help you design the massage and relaxation to suit your baby's needs. Trust yourself; you know your child better than anyone else. You are his or her specialist, and a companion in a way no one else can ever be.


## DEVELOPMENTAL IMPAIRMENTS


Developmental challenges such as cerebral palsy manifest in many different ways. The child's physical therapist will use procedures that either inhibit (relax) or facilitate (stimulate) muscle tone. Inhibition lessens muscle tone while facilitation increases it. Inhibitory techniques may include slow stroking, gentle shaking, positioning, rocking, and neutral warmth. Facilitating techniques may include icing, brushing, positioning, pressure, and vibration. The massage strokes in this book can be modified to either facilitate or inhibit; to inhibit, use long, slow, sweeping strokes and Touch Relax-

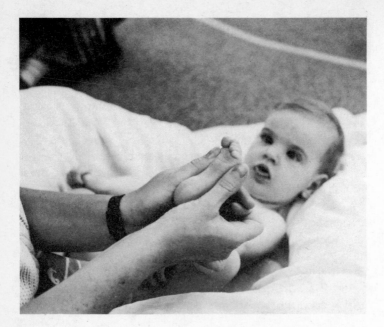

ation. To facilitate, use a more vigorous stroking and
more playful interactions such as bouncy rhymes and
songs.

   The massage can be delivered in the same order
as we show in Chapter Eight, with the following changes.
Stroking the bottom of the foot often causes the "positive supporting reaction," an extension and tighten-
ing of the leg. If this occurs, change the stroke so that
pressure is given on the outside rather than the balls
of the feet. The Thumbs to Sides stroke is particularly
helpful in improving and stimulating diaphragmatic
breathing. When doing the gas-relief routine, do not hold
the knees against the stomach for more than a count
of five, because this position can inhibit respiration in
developmentally impaired babies. Infants with developmental impairments often show signs of resistance

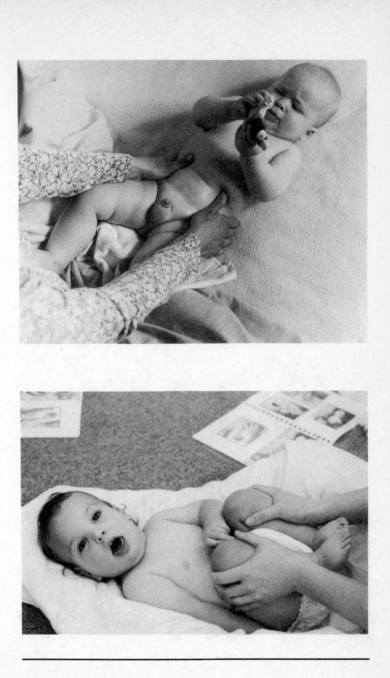

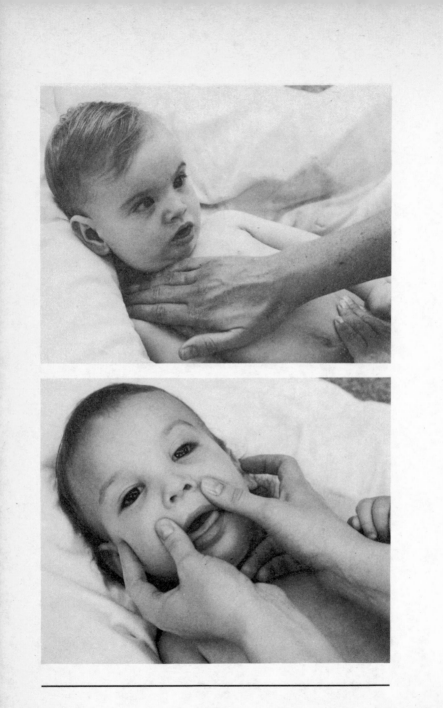

when the shoulders are stroked. Begin with just one stroke, such as the Butterfly stroke across the chest, which includes the shoulder, and gradually increase as the child's stimulation threshold rises. The strokes over the lips aid lip closure, promoting good swallowing. These are particularly good for babies who drool and breathe through the mouth. The facial massage is an excellent prelude to oral stimulation and feeding therapy for the child who is very sensitive around the mouth.

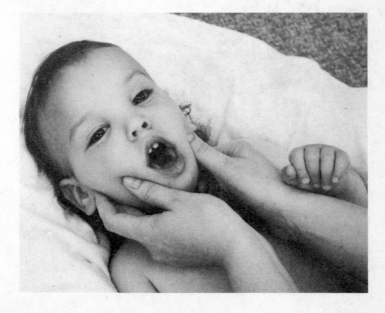

Babies who are tactile defensive, that is, hypersensitive and reactive to skin contact, benefit by firm pressure and stroking; warm baths and brisk rubbing with a terrycloth towel before massage can help increase acceptance of skin-to-skin massage. A slow firm stroke down the center of the back can increase brain organization; do not stroke up the back against hair growth.

If your baby has a shunt or other type of bypass, the strokes can be applied, working around it; your baby's physical therapist will be able to tell you how much pressure is appropriate around these areas. If your baby has had surgery, you can use massage and Touch Relaxation with other parts of his or her body; your loving touch and the security of it can be very important to your baby's recovery.

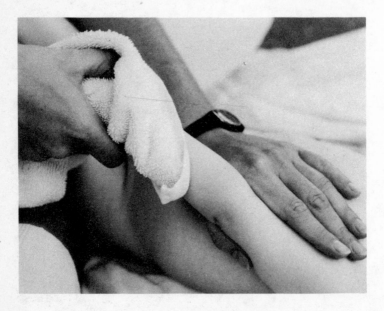

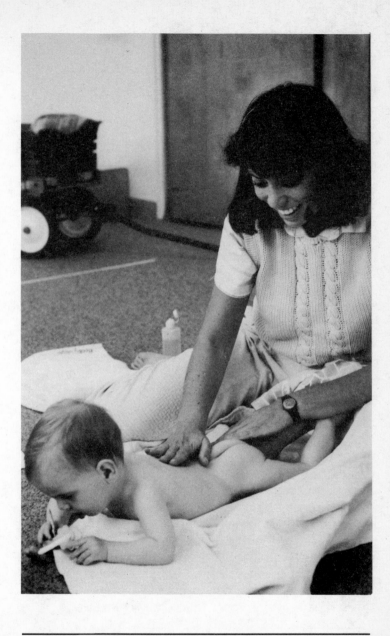

# VISUAL IMPAIRMENTS

Massage can be a particularly positive experience for visually impaired babies because of their need for tactile stimulation as a means to define their world. Researchers have found remarkable results in both animal and human babies with visual impairments when tactile stimulation is used. One study reported that visual impairment did not produce a depression of emotional and learning behavior in animals if they received touch stimulation, whereas if this kind of stimulation was withdrawn, the animals became either excessively passive or hyperaggressive. Other researchers have shown that babies in institutions who receive only twenty minutes of extra handling per day have significantly earlier development of visual attentiveness, indicating that the sensory system interlocks; the stimulation of touch does encourage visual exploration. Visually impaired infants whose parents are particularly effective in establishing emotional bonds with them show a great deal of social interaction, perceptual attentiveness, and responsiveness in the first few months of life. These babies are able to reach toward sounds earlier than other visually impaired babies.

Massage helps babies form an effective body image; this is important in establishing the object-constancy which allows the baby to let go of the parent and begin exploring the environment. The motor development of visually impaired babies in the first few months is not different from sighted babies; however, there is often a lag in the onset of crawling and walking. Some researchers suggest that this may be due to the blind infant's resistance to lying prone, which may curtail the

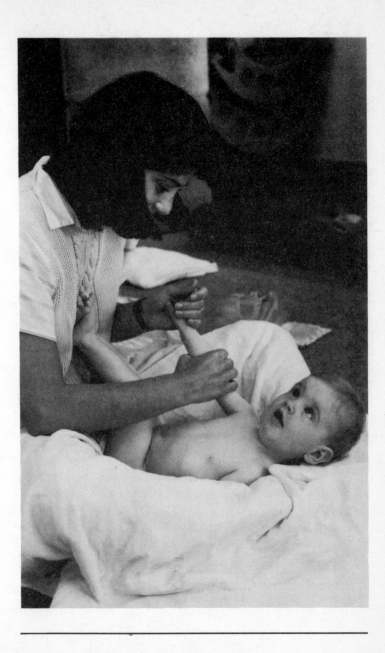

development of upper body strength which is necessary for reaching and crawling. Massage in the prone position may gradually help the baby accept this position for play because massage becomes associated with trust and safety.

Your voice and touch will simultaneously communicate love to your baby. Because you may not get the facial response you instinctively expect, you may find yourself withdrawing; instead, find ways of developing an intimate rapport with your child through touch. Talk to your baby during the massage, explaining what you are doing and telling your baby what will happen next. Use his or her name often and exaggerate auditory cues such as swishing the oil between your palms. During the first six months, do not use music or other sounds besides your voice; later, music which imitates the rhythm of the strokes can be used as long as you interact with the music in a way that connects it to the massage. Remain in close contact with your baby at all times during the massage; keep your face close, and always keep one hand on the child's body. Always begin the massage with auditory cues and by gently holding and stroking the baby's legs and feet to initiate contact. Consider the light source during the massage; light can be distracting for some partially sighted children, while others need a stronger light source to feel comfortable.

## HEARING IMPAIRMENTS

Babies with hearing impairments have the same need for tactile comfort as other babies; affectionate interaction is the most important element in any baby's life. Hearing impaired babies need to be spoken to. During this early period, sound stimulates the growth of nerve connections between the baby's ear and brain. The sound stimulation in every baby's world creates an evolving network of nerve pathways. Many hearing impaired infants are fitted with hearing aids to increase the amount of sound stimulation they receive; you can keep these on during the massage. The Infant Hearing Resource makes recommendations that might well be applied to all babies: "Tell the baby what you're thinking and feeling. He likes to hear about what makes you feel happy, sad, anxious, and excited. He can tell from the way you hold him and from your body language that you are experiencing different feelings; you might as well tell him what the names of those feelings are. Then, when he has different feelings, he'll know what to call them."

Use normal speech with your baby during massage time, and make relaxed and loving eye contact with your baby as much as possible. Describe what you're doing; for example, "This is your foot, Jason. And here are your toes. One, two, three, four, five toes!" Converse with your baby and imitate his or her sounds. Experts agree that "motherese" is a perfectly normal and acceptable form of communication with hearing impaired infants.

Massage your baby for fun and enjoyment. There are many ways that a daily massage can enrich you, too. It will help you get to know your baby better, to feel more loving toward your child, and to value his or her unique ways of communicating with the world.

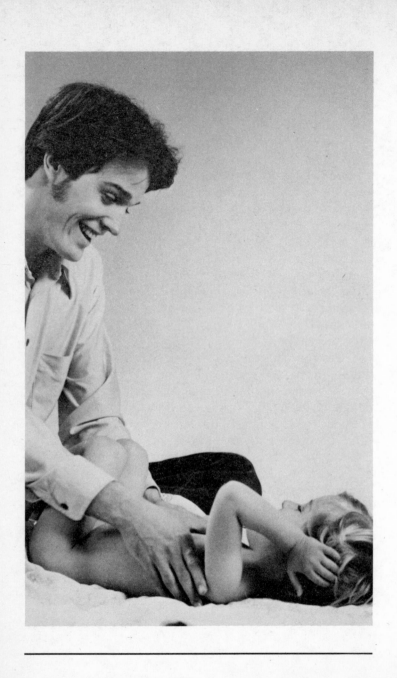

# CHAPTER THIRTEEN

# The Older Child

The plants' bright blessing springs forth
From earth's gentle being,
And human children rise up
With grateful hearts to join
The spirits of the world.

—RUDOLF STEINER

One evening after a family get-together at which a newborn cousin had made his first appearance, a friend's six-year-old daughter climbed into her mother's lap. "I wish I was a baby, Mommy," she said. "Then I'd get a lot of attention." That was a signal: time for a bedtime rubdown. Why? Not so much because she needed more attention, but because she needed to talk about the feelings her new cousin stirred in her.

It is important for children to talk about their feelings, but sometimes it's difficult to get them to open up. Often, the more we question, the more unresponsive they become. My eight-year-old was to have surgery within a week, and though I knew he should talk about his fears, I hadn't yet been able to draw him out. The day after we had taken a tour of the children's ward and met the nurses at the hospital, he seemed tense. I asked him if he had any questions. "I dunno," he mumbled, shrugging his shoulders and slinking off to his room. Later that evening I offered him a rubdown. I gently massaged his calves, knees, and feet; within five minutes he relaxed and began to talk. He had several questions about the hospital and his surgery and was finally able to get the reassurance he needed —that I'd be there with him, that he wouldn't wake up during the operation, that he would be able to talk after his tonsillectomy. The operation went smoothly and I remembered to use the soothing power of touch with him throughout the experience. A foot or hand massage now and then helped us both relax and let go of scary feelings.

Anthropologist Ashley Montague, author of *Touching*, states that a child's close relationship with his parents is a source of basic self-esteem. "Persons who are callously unresponsive to human need, who have become so hardened that they are no longer in touch with the human condition, are not merely metaphorically so," he says, "but clearly physiologically so." A study reported in the *Journal of Humanistic Psychology* confirmed this idea, indicating that the higher the subject's self-esteem, the more he communicates through touch.

Because before the age of twelve children are more tactile-kinesthetic—that is, they use feeling more than sight or hearing for information about the world—a warm touch can often trigger an outpouring of feeling or thoughts more than verbal communication. Saying "I love you" to your child is important, but more important is communicating your love through eye contact, through focused attention, and through your loving touch.

Bonding between parents and children continues. Simply because a child has graduated from the in-arms stage doesn't mean he no longer needs your attention through healthy touching. He will no longer be nursing, he won't cuddle in the same way, his circle of support will widen, and he will be increasingly busy exploring the infinite possibilities of his world. But as he grows out of his mother's and father's arms, he will come to cherish those moments of closeness that reassure him that Mommy and Daddy are always there with a warm smile and a loving massage.

Though sometime in the first nine months is the ideal time to start, it is never too late to begin the massage routine. Usually a child between one and three years of age who has not been massaged from infancy will be much too busy to be still, but you may be able to start with a short, gentle backrub at bedtime. When the child becomes accustomed to being massaged, he will begin asking for it. Before you know it, he is massaging you! Ah, the universal law of action and reaction—what you do comes full circle back to you!

## HOW TO BEGIN

Perhaps you've never considered massage as a means of opening communication lines between you and your child. How do you start without making it a "big deal"? The "Soccer Player's Special" is a good way to begin (insert any activity that may be appropriate, from ballerina to tree-climber). Here's how:

1. Make sure the area is warm and comfortable with no distractions.

2. Wash your hands and remove jewelry.

3. Bedtime or after bath is a good time, when your child is clean and ready to relax.

4. Use a natural oil, and begin by asking permission, just as we do with infants.

5. Massaging one leg at a time, use the Milking and Rolling strokes in Chapter Eight. Use your thumbs to work circles around the knees, your fingertips to gently massage calf muscles.

Ask your child for feedback: Does it feel good? Would he like it more firm, or less? Work thumbs in circles around the ankles, then in smooth strokes over the tops of the feet toward the toes. Usually, even if your child is ticklish he'll relax and talk and will forget to giggle. If he does get ticklish, just use a broader, firmer circular stroke and move back to the ankle or calf. Breathe deeply and relax, feeling warmth and deep relaxation in your hands, arms, and face. Work quietly, not expecting anything. You might, after awhile, make a statement that could draw him out such as, "You know, I was a little nervous at the hospital today. How about you?"

## STROKE AND MOVEMENT MODIFICATION

For older babies (crawling and up) some of the massage techniques must be varied somewhat to ac-

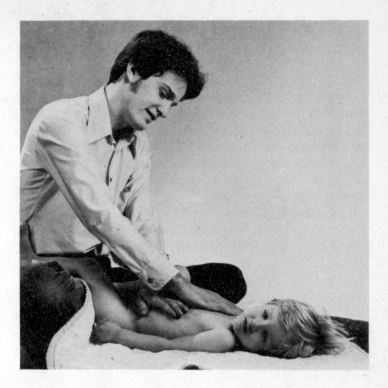

commodate the lengthening of their limbs.

Legs: The Milking stroke should be done in two parts, thigh then calf. Squeeze and Twist and Rolling should start just below the knee rather than at the hip.

Arms: The Milking strokes should be done in two parts, upper arm then forearm. Squeeze and Twist and Rolling can begin at the elbow.

Movements: The movements can be eliminated from the massage routine when your child is fully mobile. He has many opportunities to stretch and exercise his limbs and back in the course of his busy day.

# RHYMES AND GAMES FOR THE OLDER BABY

Working with an older child requires a different approach than does massaging an infant. To keep the child interested and involved, you may want to vary the massage each time, adding "zip" by means of stories, songs, and animation on your part. For instance, one of the tummy strokes most enjoyed by older children is "I Love You" (see pages 85–87). They enjoy chiming in with you as you stretch the words out, cooing in a sing-song voice. When you massage the feet, you can play "This little piggy went to market." Little games, songs, and stories that you invent as you massage your little one will involve her, entertain her active mind, and promote the kind of communication that stimulates and utilizes all of her developing senses.

## FEET AND TOES

This little piggy went to market
This little piggy stayed home
This little piggy had roast beef (tofu? pomegranates?)
This little piggy had none
This little piggy went wee wee wee wee all the way home.

One is a lady that sits in the sun;
Two is a baby and three is a nun;
Four is a lily with innocent breast;
Five is a birdie asleep in the nest.

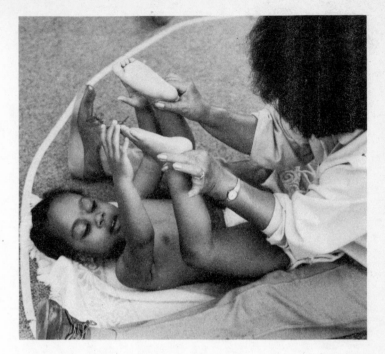

This little piggy got into the barn,
This one ate all the corn.
This one said he wasn't well,
This one said he'd go and tell,
And this one said—squeak, squeak, squeak!
I can't get over the barn door sill.

See saw, Marjorie Daw,
The hen flew over the barn.
She counted her baby chicks one by one,
    *(count each toe except the baby toe)*
But she couldn't find the little white one.
Here it is, here it is, here it is!

(Start with the little toe.)

This little cow eats grass,
This little cow eats hay,
This little cow looks over the hedge,
This little cow runs away,
And this BIG cow does nothing at all
But lie in the fields all day!
We'll chase her, and chase her,
and CHASE her!

(This rhyme goes well with the foot strokes; see number 5 and 6, page 76.)

Pitty patty polt,
Shoe the wild colt.
Here's a nail,
There's a nail,
Pitty patty polt!


TUMMY

(See Sun-Moon stroke, number 3, page 84.)

Round and round the garden
Went the teddy bear,
One step, two step, tickley under there!
    *(walk fingers up to armpit)*


FINGERS

Five little fishes swimming in a pool
    *(open hand)*

First one said, "The pool is cool"
Second one said, "The pool is deep"
Third one said, "I want to sleep"
Fourth one said, "Let's dive and dip"
Fifth one said, "I spy a ship"
They all jumped up and went ker'splash
    *(stroke top of hand)*
Away the five little fishes dash.
    *(shake hand to relax)*

(Begin with thumb.)

This is the father, short and stout
This is the mother, with children all about
This is the brother, tall you see
This is the sister with dolly on her knee
This is the baby, sure to grow
And here is the family, all in a row.

Here is a tree with leaves so green
Here are the apples that hang between
    *(hold thumb and small finger and wiggle three
    middle fingers)*
When the wind blows the apples fall
    *(hold baby's wrist and gently shake)*
And here is a basket to gather them all.
    *(cup baby's hand in yours)*

Five little kittens
All black and white
    *(cup baby's fist in your hands)*
Sleeping soundly
All through the night
Meow, meow, meow, meow, meow
    *(raise each finger)*
It's time to get up now!

---

Within a little apple
So cosy and so small
There are five little chambers
    *(cup baby's fist in your hands)*
Around a little hall.

In every room are sleeping
Two seeds of golden brown
They're lying there and dreaming
    *(open each finger and peek in)*
In beds of eiderdown.

They're dreaming there of sunshine
And how it's going to be
    *(stroke top of hand)*
When they shall hang as apples
Upon a Christmas tree.
    *(hold baby's wrist and gently shake)*


## FACE

(See pages 100–102 for strokes.)

Knock knock
    *(Open Book stroke on forehead)*
Peek in
    *(open eyes with thumbs)*
Open the latch
    *(up on nose and down across cheek with thumbs)*
And walk right in
    *(thumbs over mouth)*
Hello, Mr. Chinny-chin-chin!
    *(gently wiggle chin)*

Two little eyes to look around
Two little ears to hear each sound
One little nose to smell what's sweet
One little mouth that likes to eat.

Peek-a-boo, I see you
Hiding behind the chair
Peek-a-boo, I see you
Hiding there.

## GAMES TO PLAY WITH MOVEMENTS

ARMS

Up so high
    *(stretch arms up)*
Down so low
    *(bring arms down)*
Give a little shake
    *(shake hands at wrists)*
And hold them so.
    *(put hands together)*

This is my right arm, hold it flat
    *(hold arm out flat)*
This is my left arm, just like that
Right arm, left arm, hug myself
    *(cross arms on chest)*
Left arm, right arm,
    *(uncross and hold flat again)*
Catch a little elf!
    *(bring hands together quickly, then ask, "Did
    you catch him?" and peek in cupped hands)*

*Pat-a-cake, pat-a-cake*
      *(pat baby's hands together)*
Baker man
Bake me a cake
As fast as you can.
Roll it, and pat it
      *(roll hands around each other, and pat one with
      the other)*
And mark it with a *B*
And put it in the oven
      *(hold arms up, then down, and point to baby and
      self)*
For baby and me.


## LEGS

One leg, two legs
      *(cross over tummy)*
Hot cross buns
Right leg, left leg
      *(pull out flat)*
Isn't that fun?
      *(gently shake)*

Up
      *(knees into tummy)*
Down
      *(pull out straight)*
Up, down
Up, down
And shake them all around.

---

# HELPING AN OLDER CHILD
# ADJUST TO A NEW BABY

Through the house what busy joy,
Just because the infant boy
Has a tiny tooth to show.
I have got a double row,
All as white, and all as small;
Yet no one cares for mine at all.

—MARY LAMB

A new baby is a fascinating, fearful creature to his older brother or sister. Hovered over and protected by adults, the baby seems to be an unapproachable, somehow dangerous little being. Much has been written on the importance of letting your older child know that he is still loved and cherished in his own right when a new baby comes into the family. The next step is to help the older child and the baby to begin a relationship of their own. It usually takes quite a bit longer for a child to fully "bond" with a new sibling. His first task is to understand that the baby is "here," that mother is all right, that he is still loved as much as before, and that life goes on.

As you massage your baby every day, your older child will occasionally observe. He may remember being massaged (in fact he may still enjoy being massaged) and identify with the baby. They share an experience, have something in common.

If your child is given the opportunity to massage the baby occasionally (only if he wants to, of course), he will benefit by it in many ways, as will baby. The older child will bond with the baby in the same ways that

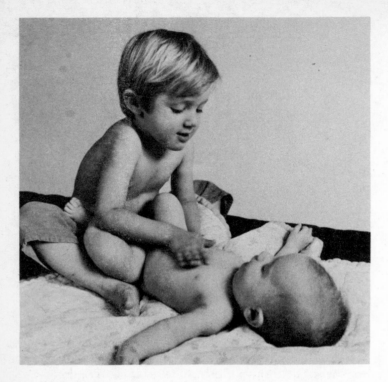

you do—with eye contact, touch, movement, sound. He will learn that baby is not necessarily so dangerous and fragile, but a person like himself. His confidence will bloom as he comes to realize his own competence as a caretaker and protector. The baby will respond to him, overcoming her initial fear of his sometimes clumsy, rough handling or startling behavior. She will begin to relate to him as a loving peer and ally.

It is best to delay suggesting that an older child massage the new baby until the baby has passed that stage of fragility when she is easily startled. Usually three or four months of age is about the right time, though a little earlier may be appropriate for an older child who is over four. Don't worry about the method or whether or not the child uses oil. You can show him a couple of things (the Open Book stroke on the chest is best, see page 89) and then let him do it as he pleases. He will at first be hesitant and may need your encouragement to touch the baby. He will probably storke the baby only a couple of times. But even the tiniest amount of contact will be very beneficial. Be sure to express your pleasure and pride to your child; let him know that he did a good job and that his massaging is valuable to the baby.

## HEALTHY TOUCHING

Parents are concerned about the touching their children receive, and how to help their children protect themselves from unhealthy individuals who may take advantage of them. Unfortunately, because of the fear engendered by newspaper stories of molested children, many parents are giving their children frightening, negative messages about touch.

It is important that our children know the difference between healthy and unhealthy touching. Infant massage is a great way to positively teach a child the difference. A child massaged from infancy has several advantages over the child who is simply educated or warned about unhealthy touches. The masssaged child knows what healthy, loving touch feels like. Because of the emotional bonds it produces between parent and child, he feels close to his parents and tends to talk about his feelings more often. Thus, he would be much more likely to report to his parents if he is concerned about the way someone talks to or touches him. In addition, massage time becomes "talking time," a time when parent and child can discuss things that are important to both of them. It is a perfect opportunity to talk about touching with your child and to help him learn how to protect himself. The type of interaction afforded by regular massage and Touch Relaxation helps your child develop a positive self-image and a sense of ownership of his body; he also develops a keen awareness of feelings and body language.

In general, massaged children grow up feeling confident and comfortable with their bodies and they openly communicate with their parents. It's a tradition with long-term benefits, and it is definitely worth the effort!

# References

---

## Chapter One

---

Page

1—Zborowsky, M., and Herzog, E. 1952. *Life Is With People.*
New York: International Univ. Press.

2—Leiderman, L.; Tulkin, S.; and Rosenfeld, A; eds. 1977. *Culture and Infancy: Variations in the Human Experience.*
New York: Academic Press.

2—Montague, A. 1978. *Touching.* New York: Harper & Row.

2—Prescott, J. 1975, Apr. "Pleasure/Violence Reciprocity Theory: The Distribution of 49 Cultures, Relating Infant Physical Affection to Adult Physical Violence." *The Futurist.*

4—Montague, A. 1978. *Touching.* New York: Harper & Row.

4—Taylor, R., prod. *The Baby Massage Movie.* (Interview with Ashley Montague.) Boulder, Colo.: Ron Taylor Films.

5—Crockenberg, S. 1981. "Infant Irritability, Mother Responsiveness, and Social Support Influences in the Security of Infant-Mother Attachment." *Child Development,* Vol. 52.

5—Devore, I., et al. 1974. *Ethology and Psychiatry.* Toronto: Univ. of Toronto Press.

5—Fitzgerald, H., et al. 1982. *Child Nurturance: Studies of Development in Non-human Primates.* [Vol. III]. New York: Plenum.

5—Harlow, H. 1958. "The Nature of Love." *American Psychologist,* Vol. 13.

5—Harlow, H. 1959, June. "Love in Infant Monkeys." *Scientific American.*

5—Harlow, H., and Harlow, M. 1962, Nov. "Social Deprivation in Monkeys." *Scientific American.*

---

6—Harlow, H.; Harlow, M.; Dodsworth R.; and Arling, G. 1966. "Maternal Behavior of Rhesus Monkeys Deprived of Mothering and Peer Association in Infancy." *Proceedings of the American Philosophical Society,* Vol. 110.

6—Montague, A. 1978. *Touching.* New York: Harper & Row.

6—Hammett, F. 1921. "Studies in the Thyroid Apparatus: I." *American Journal of Physiology,* Vol. 56.

6—Hammett, F. 1922. "Studies of the Thyroid Apparatus: V." *Endocrinology,* Vol. 6.

6—Montague, A. 1978. *Touching.* New York: Harper & Row.

7—Field, T.; Schanberg, S.; Scafidi, F.; Bauer, C.; Vega-Lahr, N.; Garcia, R.; Nystrom, J.; and Kuhn, C. 1986, May. "Tactile/Kinesthetic Stimulation Effects on Preterm Neonates." *Pediatrics,* Vol. 77.

7—Rice, R. 1977. "Neurophysiological Development in Premature Infants Following Stimulation." *Developmental Psychology,* Vol. 13.

7–8—Epstein, H. 1974. "Phrenoblysis: Special Brain and Mind Growth Periods." *Developmental Psychobiology.* New York: Wiley.

8—Reinis, S., and Goldman, J. 1980. *The Development of the Brain.* Springfield, Ill.: Thomas.

8—Rorke, L., and Riggs, H. 1969. *Myelination of the Brain in the Newborn.* Philadelphia: Lippincott.

8—Brown, C., ed. 1984. *The Many Facets of Touch.* (Johnson and Johnson Pediatric Round Table No. 10.) New York: Elsevier.

8—Restak, R. 1986. *The Infant Mind.* New York: Doubleday.

8—Montague, A. 1978. *Touching.* New York: Harper & Row.

9—Pearce, J. 1977. *Magical Child.* New York: Dutton.

9—Selye, H. 1974. *Stress Without Distress.* New York: New American Library.

10—Witkin-Lanoil, G. 1984. *The Female Stress Syndrome.* New York: Berkley Books.

12—Clary, E., et al. 1986. "Socialization and Situational Influences on Sustained Altruism." *Child Development,* Vol. 57.

12—Goleman, D. 1985, Sept. 10. "Patterns of Love Charted in Studies." [Childhood ties bind us to the future.] *New York Times.*

12—Roberts, M. 1987, Mar. "Baby Love." [Effects of infant experience on later adult love life; a study by Shaver and Hazan.] *Psychology Today.*

# Chapter Two

Page

15—Hooker, D. 1952. *The Prenatal Origins of Behavior.* Lawrence, Kan.: Univ. of Kansas Press.

15–16—Liley, A. 1972. "The Fetus as a Personality." *Australian and New Zealand Journal of Psychiatry,* Vol. 6.

16—Hunziker, U., and Barr, R. 1986, May. "Increased Carrying Reduces Infant Crying: A Randomized Control Trial. *Pediatrics,* Vol. 77.

16—Porter, R., et al. 1983, Fall. "The Importance of Odors in Mother-Infant Interactions." *Maternal Child Nursing,* Vol. 12.

16—McCarthy, P. 1986, July. "Scent: The Tie That Binds?" *Psychology Today.*

17—Bernhardt, J. 1987, Jan.-Feb. "Sensory Capabilities of the Fetus." *Maternal Child Nursing,* Vol. 12.

17—Restak, R. 1986. *The Infant Mind.* New York: Doubleday.

17–18—Bower, T. 1966, Dec. "The Visual World of Infants." *Scientific American.* Vol. 215.

18—Fantz, R. 1962. "Maturation of Pattern Vision in Young Infants." *Journal of Comparative and Physiological Psychology,* Vol. 55.

18—Fantz, R. 1963. "Pattern Vision in Newborn Infants." *Science,* Vol. 140.

18–19—DeCasper, A., et al. 1980, June 6. "Of Human Bonding: Newborns Prefer Their Mothers' Voices." *Science,* Vol. 208.

18—Klaus, M., and Kennell, J. 1983. *Bonding: The Beginning of Parent-Infant Attachment.* New York: New American Library.

18—Restak, R. 1986. *The Infant Mind.* New York: Doubleday.

18—DeCasper, A., et al. 1980, June 6. "Of Human Bonding: Newborns Prefer Their Mothers' Voices." *Science,* Vol. 208.

18—Restak, R. 1986. *The Infant Mind.* New York: Doubleday.

18–19—Condon, W., and Sander, L. 1974, June. "Neonate Movement Is Synchronized With Adult Speech: Interactional

Participation and Language Acquisition." *Science,* Vol. 183.

19—Springer, S., and Deutsch, G. 1985. *Left Brain, Right Brain.* New York: Freeman.

19—Ludington-Hoe, S. 1985. *How to Have a Smarter Baby.* New York: Rawson Assoc.

20–21—Williams, H. 1987. In personal interview with Vimala McClure.

# Chapter Three

Page

23—D'Spagnat, B. 1979, Nov. "The Quantum Theory and Reality." *Scientific American.*

23—Capra, F. 1980. *The Tao of Physics.* New York: Bantam Books.

23–24—Pearce, J. 1986. *Magical Child Matures.* New York: Bantam Books.

24—Lorenz, K. 1965. *Evolution and the Modification of Behavior.* Chicago: Univ. of Chicago Press.

24—Harlow, H., and Harlow, M. 1959. "Learning to Love." *American Scientist,* Vol. 54.

24—Harlow, H.; Harlow, M.; and Hansen, E. 1963. *Maternal Behavior in Mammals.* New York: Wiley.

24—Harlow, H., and Harlow, M. 1969. "Effects of Various Mother-Infant Relationships on Rhesus Monkey Behaviors." In *Determinants of Infant Behavior,* B.M. Foss, ed., Vol. 4. London: Methuen.

24—Klaus, M., and Kennell, J. 1967. *Maternal Infant Bonding.* St. Louis: Mosby.

25—Magid, K., and McKelvey, C. 1987. *High Risk: Children Without a Conscience.* New York: Bantam Books.

25–26—Klaus, M., and Kennell, J. 1982. *Parent Infant Bonding.* St. Louis: Mosby.

27—Pearce, J. 1986. *Magical Child Matures.* New York: Bantam Books.

28—Restak, R. 1986. *The Infant Mind.* New York: Doubleday.

32—Zigler, E. 1985, Oct. 17. "Recommendations of the Yale Bush Center Advisory Committee on Infant Care Leave." *Hearing on parental leave HR 2020 before House Subcommittees on civil service, labor management relations, labor standards, and employee benefits.*

32—Magid, K., and McKelvey, C. 1987. *High Risk: Children Without a Conscience.* New York: Bantam Books.

# Chapter Four

Page

36, 38—Daly, T. 1987, Winter. "Men, Infant Massage, and Manhood." *Tender Loving Care* (newsletter): International Association of Infant Massage Instructors.

38–39—Lamb, M. 1981. *The Role of the Father in Child Development.* New York: Wiley.

39—Block, J. 1971. *Lives Through Time.* Berkeley, Ca.: Bancroft Books.

39—Lozoff, M. 1974. "Fathers and Autonomy in Women." In *Women and Success,* Kundsin, R., ed. New York: Morrow.

# Chapter Seven

Page

59—Wolff, P. 1965. "The Causes, Controls, and Organization of Behavior in the Neonate." *Psychological Issues* [Monograph 17], Vol 5.

59–60—Glas, N. 1972. *Conception, Birth, and Early Childhood.* Spring Valley, New York: Anthroposophic Press.

63—Davis, A. 1972. *Let's Have Healthy Children.* New York: Harcourt Brace Jovanovich.

# Chapter Eight

Page

75—Berkson, D. 1977. *The Foot Book: Healing With the Integrated Treatment of Foot Reflexology.* New York: Funk & Wagnalls.

# Chapter Eleven

Page

142—Field, T., et al. 1986, May. "Tactile/Kinesthetic Stimulation Effects on Preterm Neonates." *Pediatrics,* Vol. 77.

142—Field, T., et al. 1979, July. "Cardiac and Behavioral Responses to Repeated Tactile and Auditory Stimulation of Preterm and Term Neonates." *Developmental Psychology,* Vol. 15.

142—Gottfried, A., et al. 1980, Mar. "Touch as an Organizer for Learning and Development." In *The Many Facets of Touch,* Brown, C., ed. (Johnson and Johnson Pediatric Round Table No. 10.) New York: Elsevier.

142—Kramer, M., et al. 1975, Sept.-Oct. "Extra Tactile Stimulation of the Premature Infant." *Nursing Research,* Vol. 24.

142—Oehler, J. 1985, Feb. "The Development of the Preterm Infant's Responsiveness to Auditory and Tactile Social Stimuli." *Dissertation Abstracts,* Vol. 45(8B).

142—Rausch, P. 1984. "A Tactile and Kinesthetic Stimulation Program for Premature Infants." In *The Many Facets of Touch,* Brown, C., ed. (Johnson and Johnson Pediatric Round Table No. 10.) New York: Elsevier.

142—Rice, R. 1977. "Neurophysiological Development in Premature Infants Following Stimulation." *Developmental Psychology,* Vol 13.

142—Schaeffer, J. 1982. "The Effects of Gentle Human Touch on Mechanically Ventilated Very Short Gestation Infants." *Maternal Child Nursing* [Monograph 12], Vol. 11.

142—White, J., et al. 1976, Nov. "The Effects of Tactile and Kinesthetic Stimulation on Neonatal Development in the Premature Infant." *Developmental Psychobiology,* Vol. 9.

147—Grossmann, K., et al. 1981, Mar. "Maternal Tactual Contact of the Newborn After Various Postpartum Conditions of Mother-Infant Contact." *Developmental Psychology,* Vol. 17.

147—Powell, L. 1974, Mar. "The Effect of Extra Stimulation and Maternal Involvement on the Development of Low Birthweight Infants and on Maternal Behavior." *Child Development,* Vol. 45.

142,—Rose, S. 1984. "Preterm Responses to Passive, Active, and
150    Social Touch." In *The Many Facets of Touch,* Brown, C., ed. (Johnson and Johnson Pediatric Round Table No. 10.) New York: Elsevier.

# Chapter Twelve

Page

159—Fraser, B. 1986. "Child Impairment and Parent-Infant
−160   Communication." *Child Care, Health, and Development,* Vol. 12.

160—Harrison, H. 1983. *The Premature Baby Book.* New York: St. Martin's Press.

160—Simons, R. 1985. *After the Tears: Parents Talk About Raising a Child With a Disability.* Denver, Colo.: Children's
Museum of Denver.

160—Speirer, J. 1982. *Infant Massage for Developmentally De-
-166 layed Babies.* Denver, Colo.: United Cerebral Palsy Center.

166—Ayres, J. 1979. *Sensory Integration and the Child.* Los
Angeles: Western Psychological Services.

168—Riesen, A. 1966. "Sensory Deprivation." In *Progress in Physiological Psychology,* Stellar, E., and Sprague, J., eds.
New York: Academic Press.

168—White, B., and Held, R. 1966. "Plasticity of Sensorimotor
Development in the Human Infant." In *Causes of Behavior: Readings in Child Development and Educational
Psychology* (2nd ed.), Rosenblith, J., and Allinsmith, W.,
eds. Boston: Allyn and Bacon.

168—Bigelow, A. 1988, Nov. "The Development of Reaching in
Blind Infants." *British Journal of Developmental
Psychology,* Vol. 4.

168—Cratty, B., and Sams, T. 1968. *The Body Image of Blind
Children.* New York: American Foundation for the Blind.

168—Warren, D. 1984. *Blindness and Early Childhood Development.* New York: American Foundation for the Blind.

168—Hart, V. 1983. "Characteristics of Young Blind Children."
Paper presented at the Second International Sympo-
sium on Visually Handicapped Infants and Young Children: Birth to 7. Aruba.

171—Infant Hearing Resource. 1985. *Parent-Infant Communication: A Program of Clinical and Home Training for
Parents and Hearing Impaired Infants.* Portland, Ore.: Infant Hearing Resource.

# ADDITIONAL REFERENCES

Ainsworth, M. 1967. *Infancy in Uganda.* Baltimore: Johns Hop-
kins Univ. Press.

Altmann, M. 1963. *Maternal Behavior in Mammals.* New York:
Wiley.

Aries, P. 1962. *Centuries of Childhood.* New York: Knopf.

Ayres, J. 1979. *Sensory Integration and the Child.* Los Angeles:

Western Psychological Services.

Bowlby, J. 1969. *Attachment and Loss.* New York: Basic Books.

Briggs, D. 1975. *Your Child's Self-Esteem.* Garden City, N.Y.: Doubleday.

Carpenter, E. 1973. *Eskimo Realities.* New York: Holt, Rinehart & Winston.

Cass-Beggs, B. 1978. *Your Baby Needs Music.* New York: St. Martin's Press.

Crelin, E. 1973. *Functional Anatomy of the Newborn.* New Haven, Conn.: Yale Univ. Press.

Daikin, L. 1959. *The Lullaby Book.* London: Publications Ltd.

Geestesleven, U. 1966. *Clump-a-Dump and Snickle-Snack: Pentatonic Songs for Children.* Spring Valley, N.Y.: Mercury Press.

Gubernick, D. 1981. *Parental Care in Mammals.* New York: Plenum.

Haynes, U. 1983. *Holistic Health Care for Children With Developmental Disabilities.* Baltimore: University Park Press.

Hunt, D. 1970. *Parents and Children in History.* New York: Basic Books.

Infant Hearing Resource. 1985. *Parent Infant Communication: A Program of Clinical and Home Training for Parents and Hearing Impaired Infants.* Portland, Ore.: Infant Hearing Resource.

Jones, S. 1983. *Crying Baby, Sleepless Nights.* New York: Warner Books.

Matterson, E. 1972. *This Little Puffin.* London: Penguin Books.

Neurnberger, P. 1981. *Freedom From Stress.* Honesdale, Pa.: Himalayan Institute.

Ogden, L. 1982. *The Silent Garden: Understanding the Hearing Impaired Child.* New York: St. Martin's Press.

Opie, I., and Opie, P. 1955. *The Oxford Nursery Rhyme Book.* London: Oxford Univ. Press.

Osofsky, J. 1979. *Handbook of Infant Development.* New York: Wiley.

Parke, R. 1978. "Parent-Infant Interaction: Progress, Paradigms, and Problems." In *Observing Behavior: Theory and Applications in Mental Retardation.* Baltimore: University Park Press.

Queen, S., and Habenstein, R. 1961. *The Family in Various Cultures.* New York: Lippincott.

Samuels, M., and Samuels, N. 1979. *The Well Baby Book.* New York: Simon & Schuster.

Sears, W. 1985. *The Fussy Baby.* Franklin Park, Ill.: La Leche League Intl.

Solter, A. 1984. *The Aware Baby.* Goleta, Ca.: Shining Star Press.

---

Speirer, J. 1982. *Infant Massage for Developmentally Delayed Babies.* Denver, Colo.: United Cerebral Palsy Center.

Steele, S. 1985, July-August. "Young Children With Cerebral Palsy: Practical Guidelines for Care." *Pediatric Nursing.*

Strauss, L. 1982, Apr. "The Effects of Tactile Stimulation on the Communicative, Social-Emotional, and Motor Behaviors of Deaf-Blind-Multihandicapped Infants. *Dissertation Abstracts,* Vol. 42(10A).

Verney, T., and Kelly, J. 1981. *The Secret Life of the Unborn Child.* New York: Dell.

Warren, D. 1984. *Blindness and Early Childhood Development.* New York: American Foundation for the Blind.

# ABOUT THE AUTHOR

**Vimala Schneider McClure** lives with her husband and three children in the Ozark Mountains of southern Missouri. Her work with parents and babies since 1976 led her to found the International Association of Infant Massage Instructors. For information about infant massage classes, home visits, instructor training, and inservices for professionals contact:

The International Association
of Infant Massage Instructors
P.O. Box 16103
Portland, OR 97216

794

9013